Flora mcdonald

From a painting by Allan Ramsay.
Facsimile autograph from an original letter.

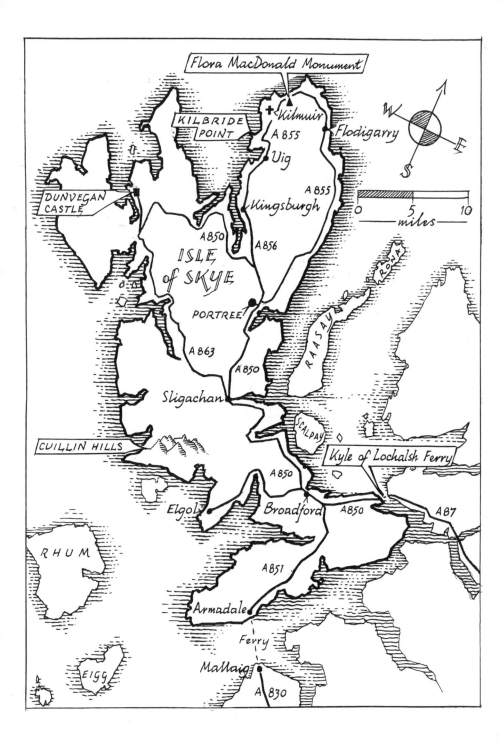

THE
FLORA MACDONALD
STORY

By
Alexander MacGregor

Published in 1989 by Lang Syne Publishers, Old School, Blanefield, Glasgow, and printed by Waterside Printers.
Copyright LANG SYNE PUBLISHERS LTD 1989.
ISBN : 185 217 145 6

This is a condensed re-issue of the Life of Flora MacDonald by Alexander MacGregor, first published by Eneas Mackay of Stirling.

INTRODUCTION

Bonnie Prince Charlie's campaign to, become King of Great Britain ended in disaster on the bloody battlefield of Culloden Moor.

And for months afterwards he was a fugitive, hunted by Government troops across the Highlands and Islands of Scotland.

Although a huge reward, worth £750,000 in today's terms, was offered for information that would lead to his arrest not a single Highlander betrayed the young Charles Edward Stuart.

In fact many risked their lives and those of their families by helping him to escape. And of this brave and gallant band the most daring was a young woman called Flora MacDonald.

It was Flora, then just 24, who disguised the Prince as her Irish spinning maid Betty Burke and smuggled him out of Scotland under the noses of thousands of English redcoats.

This is the true story of that remarkable rescue mission — a mission that was to make 'Flora's' name famous around the world.

Keeping as closely as possible to the original famous biography of Flora by Alexander MacGregor M.A., first published more than a century ago, the great value of this work lies in the fact that it is based on first hand information which he obtained from Flora's daughter, Anne. She married Major-General Alexander Macleod and lived at Stein in Skye until her death in 1834.

After dealing with the circumstances surrounding the Rebellion and its aftermath the book follows Flora to her new life in America where her family were caught up in the Wars of Independence.

But her last days were spent in Scotland and her funeral, second only after her wedding, was the largest attended public event ever seen in the Western Isles.

Diary of Flora MacDonald

1722. Flora is born at Milton, South Uist. Charles Edward Stuart was then a two-year old.

1724. Her father, Ranald MacDonald, dies.

1728. Her mother marries Hugh MacDonald of Kingsburgh, Skye.

1745. Charles raises the Standard at Glenfinnan on August 19 and the Rebellion begins.

1746. His dream dies at Culloden on April 16. A few weeks later, on June 20, Flora meets the Prince near her birthplace at Milton, South Uist. Four days later, after a second meeting, they go by open boat from Rossinish to Kilbride in Skye, more than 40 miles away.

On July 1 they part forever. On July 12 Flora is arrested and kept prisoner on the navy ship Furnace.

September 20: Charles leaves Scotland never to return.

November 20: After a term of imprisonment in Edinburgh Flora arrives by ship in London where she is detained for a further eight months.

1747. On July 4 Flora, then 28, is released from prison.

1750. On November 6 Flora marries Allan MacDonald of Kingsburgh at Armadale, Skye and they go to have seven children.

1774. Flora, then 54, Allan and two of their sons emigrate to North Carolina, then British territory.

1776. They help raise more than 500 Highlanders to fight for Britain in the American Wars of Independence.

February 27: Allan captured at the Battle of Moore's Creek and jailed for 18 months.

1780. July: Her days as an emigrant over, Flora is back in Skye, at Dunvegan.

1784. Her husband returns to Skye. They had been apart for six years.

1787. They set up what is perhaps their first real settled home at Penduin near Kingsburgh.

1790. Flora dies on March 4, two years after Prince Charles had passed on in Rome. She was 68. Her shroud was one of the sheets used by the Prince to keep warm while on the run.

1792. Flora's husband dies at Kingsburgh and is buried alongside his wife at Kilmuir.

Fiery Cross over mountain and glen

The circumstances of the Rebellions of 1715 and 1745 are well documented in the pages of Scotland's story.

James the Sixth of Scotland and First of England was the common ancestor of the two families which fought for the throne of Great Britain. He was succeeded in 1625 by Charles I who was beheaded twenty-four years later.

His son, Charles II, after the death of Cromwell, was placed on the throne, in 1660. Having died without fathering an heir, his brother, the Duke of York, under the title of James II, succeeded him in 1685. His reign, however, was short. He was dethroned four years later because of his religion and forced to leave the kingdom.

His daughter, Mary, with William, grandson of Charles I, then succeeded to the throne. After them, Queen Anne, another daughter of James II, began to reign.

She died without issue in 1714, leaving behind her a brother named James. This James, being of course the son of James II, is well known in history as the Pretender, or the Chevalier St George.

He had naturally a keen eye to the kingdom, and was strongly supported by several powerful friends. Among those most devoted to his cause was the Earl of Mar, who had forces of coniderable strength in readiness for action. Possessed himself of no small number of willing retainers, he had the benefit of numerous allies from France.

James, with no doubt of success, unfurled his banner at Braemar, in the Highlands of Aberdeenshire, in 1715, but was defeated soon after at Sheriffmuir. Like his father, James II, he was banished from Britain.

Amid all these bloody insurrections, the Parliament of the nation bestowed the crown on the nearest Protestant heir,

George, Elector of Hanover, and great-grandson of James I. This monarch, styled George I, died in 1727, and was succeeded by his son, George II.

In the meantime James, the Chevalier St George, had married Clementina, grandaughter of John Sobieski, the heroic King of Poland, by whom he had a son, Charles Edward, born in 1720, and hero of the Rebellion of 1745.

The Chevalier St George is said to have been a man of little judgment, and of weak and vacillating character. But, on the other hand, the blood of Sobieski seems to have invigorated his son, Charles Edward, with greater mental powers, and to have inspired him with that courage, which in 1745-6 almost enabled him to retrieve the fortunes of his family.

A lad of just 25 summers, he landed in the Highlands of Scotland, utterly unprepared for his hazardous adventure. He had no army, no money and no munitions when he found himself in a lonely, sequestered corner of the West Highlands, in the midst of strangers, and with only seven attendants.

Yet his aim was to regain the Crown of Great Britain, already possessed by a near relative; and which had been lost to his own family for fifty-seven years!

To the wise, this enterprise could scarcely fail to appear as a forlorn hope — yet by his amiable manners and captivating address the Prince soon enlisted the feelings and services of the majority of the Highland clans.

News of his arrival spread with the telegraphy of the 'fiery cross' over mountain and glen. The Highlanders were on the alert. Under the guardianship of their brave chiefs they soon hied to the general rendezvous, where a halo of glory seemed to overshadow their arms, and a confidence of success inspire their hearts!

The youthful Prince placed himself at the head of no insignificant body. His soldiers were, no doubt, untrained, and unskilled in the more scientific modes of carrying on a great war, but they possessed all the qualities which go to make good soldiers; their valour and endurance were great.

It is well known that with these untutored but devoted followers, the Prince took possession of Scotland, penetrated

England as far as Derby, and caused His Majesty, King George II to tremble on his throne!

Had he boldly entered London, as he had done our Scottish towns, it is difficult to say what the result might have been; but for various reasons he retreated to the Highlands for the winter, rather than advance, although he was within a hundred miles of London.

From that moment the prospects of the prince began to look gloomy. His star began to wane, until on April 16, 1746, it was completely extinguished on the bloody moor of Culloden!

On that ill-selected field his army was broken to pieces by the well-trained forces of the Duke of Cumberland. His brave Highlanders fell in hundreds by his side, and he himself became a fugitive and outlaw in the land of his Royal ancestors.

Escaping from the scene of slaughter and defeat, he withdrew, with all possible speed, to the western parts of the county of Inverness, in the hope of escaping by sea to France. In this he was, however, for a time unsuccessful.

At Moy Hall, the residence of the Mackintosh of Mackintosh, within twelve miles of Inverness, the Prince narrowly escaped falling into the hands of the enemy. The chief of Mackintosh himself was loyal to the Government, and was greatly guided in his movements by his neighbour, President Forbes of Culloden.

Lady Mackintosh, on the other hand, like many others of her sex, favoured the Prince. By her influence she had privately induced many of her clan to support the cause.

The Government put a price of £30,000 on the Prince's head! Such a sum in those days was enormous wealth, especially in the eyes of a poor Highlander; yet not one was found sufficiently mean to betray him.

Charles, shaken by the unexpected turn of events, lost no time in setting off for a place of safety. Having provided a considerable body of horse, as well as several foot soldiers, he departed along with Sir Thomas Sheridan, Captain O'Neill, Mr John Hay, Mr O'Sullivan, a faithful old Highlander named Edward Burke, who acted as a guide, and several others.

They crossed the River Nairn between three and four miles from Culloden, by one of General Wade's bridges. Here the Prince halted to consult his friends as to what should be done.

The Highland chiefs who had backed him still expected that they might be able to succeed. It was, however, apparent that the Prince did not at heart sympathise with the plans of those who had already sacrificed so much for his cause.

'His wish was,' says noted Jacobite historian William Chambers, 'to make his way as quickly as possible to France, in order to use personal exertions in procuring those powerful supplies which had been so much and so vainly wished for.

'He expected to find French vessels hovering on the West Coast, in one of which he might obtain a quick passage to that country. He had therefore decided to proceed in this direction without loss of time.'

The country Charles and his party crossed was deplorably desolated. Dwelling-houses and cottages were deserted by their inmates, who had fled to the rocks and mountains for shelter from the reputed cruelty of the enemy.

The party, crushed with fatigue and hunger, arrived at the steading of Tordarroch, but found it shut up. They then wandered on to Aberarder, which was also abandoned.

From Aberarder they moved along to Farraline House, where they fared no better. At length with much ado, they reached Gorthlig House, the residence of Mr Thomas Fraser, then acting as manager and factor for Lord Lovat. It happened at this time that Simon, Lord Lovat, resided at his factor's house, and very likely made a point of being present on that memorable day, as by his instructions, a great feast was being prepared to celebrate the expected victory of the Prince at Culloden.

How crest-fallen Lovat must have been when the Prince told him the sad news.

Various accounts are given of the effects it produced on the aged chief. It is said that he became frantic with alarm, and fled to the field beyond the dwelling, exclaiming 'Cut my head off at once! Chop it off; chop it off.' By another account, he is represented as having 'received the Prince with expressions of attachment, but reproached him severely for his intention of abandoning the enterprise.'

The Prince having thus passed a few hours in conversation with his lordship, then set off to Invergarry, the romantic stronghold of Macdonald of Glengarry. They arrived there a little before sunrise, and found everything wearing a most cheerless aspect.

The great halls of the castle, which often resounded with the shrill notes of the piobaireachd, and lavished their hospitality on high and low, were desolate and empty. The castle had been completely dismantled, the furniture removed, the walls made bare, and the whole fabric appeared the emblem of desolation and ruin!

One solitary individual was found in this once lordly mansion, but he had nothing to give to the weary wanderers to refresh them, but some fish to eat, and the hard, cold floor for a bed.

They all slept, however, for several hours in their clothes, but on awaking from their unrefreshing repose, the whole party deemed it prudent to take leave of the Prince, with the exception of O'Neil, O'Sullivan, and Burke.

Later that morning the Prince received a long communication from Lord George Murray, dated Ruthven, detailing the numerous blunders that had been committed, and stating that various chiefs, with an assembled army of between two and three thousand men, were ready to relaunch the campaign. The Prince sent back a message requesting the army to immediately disperse.

'In thus resigning the contest', says the chronicler, 'which, by his inconsiderate rashness, he had provoked, Charles showed that he was possessed of that magnaminity which many of his followers ascribed to him.'

On the evening of the same day Prince Charles and his small party left Glengarry's inhospitable mansion, and travelled to Loch Arkaig, in the country of the Camerons. They arrived late at night at Clunes, where everything possible was done for their comfort.

Old Cameron of Clunes had been an officer in Lochiel's regiment, and was killed at Prestonpans, fighting bravely for his Prince. His son and heir, Young Clunes, felt much for the misfortunes that lately befell the Prince's cause, and devised a plan for his safety.

Cheese and whisky for fugitives in a cave

A secure and suitable cave was fitted up comfortably for the use of his Royal Highness and friends. Provisions were furnished for the occasion, and to entertain the party well, Clunes killed an ox and ordered a portion of it to be immediately dressed and carried to the cave where the fugitives were concealed.

Besides all this, a substantial supply of bread, cheese and whisky was forwarded with the other viands, which was, no doubt, found very acceptable.

When it was necessary to depart, Clunes provided a boat for the fugitives, and Lochiel, who ventured to accompany them a part of the way. The boat was the only one in the district, all the rest had been burnt to prevent the rebels from using them.

Lochiel and the Prince hesitated to cross the Lochy in the fragile craft, but Clunes at once volunteered to cross first with a batch of his friends, and, having done so safely, the Prince and his party followed his example.

In momentary terror that their route would be discovered, they made all haste to reach Glenbiasdale. They arrived late in the evening of Saturday, April 19, at the head of Loch Morar, where they remained as darkness had come on, and the night promised to be wild and wet.

They could find no human dwelling to take shelter in until at last one of the party stumbled upon a lonely little hovel in the corner of a wood, which had been used at the sheep shearing. There was no seat, table, nor stool in it, but Burke contrived to kindle a fire with turfs which lay in a corner, and having made seats of stones, the party passed the night as well as they could.

As there was no boat at Loch Morar to ferry them across, they had no alternative but to walk round it on foot, and to cross steep and rugged ranges of mountains to accomplish their journey, which they did with great difficulty, arriving at Arisaig in the evening.

The Prince knew that he was in great danger. Time was rapidly slipping away, and the vigilant enemy were getting closer with every passing hour.

A council was held as to what ought to be done. It was the Prince's own wish to go to the Outer Hebrides, but his friends sternly objected, giving as a reason that Government cruisers had already been ordered to scour all the lochs, bays, and channels of these regions. The chance of his being seized was much greater than if he remained on the mainland.

The meeting pondered in deep suspense, and their almost unanimous decision nearly prevailed on the Prince to remain where he was, under the protectoin of his kind and faithful adherents.

O'Sullivan alone objected, and eloquently insisted on the propriety of resorting to the Isles. He strenuously maintained that this was the only way of finding a ship to France.

Some of the others present, however, were highly critical of the plan and accused O'Sullivan of having grossly mismanaged the campaign and tactics at Culloden.

In the midst of all this the Prince was informed that Donald Macleod, a known and trusted boatman from Skye, had fortunately arrived with his vessel at Kinlochmoidart. He would be the man to ferry them to the Hebrides.

Chambers, in his study of the Rebellion, states that a message was sent to Kinlochmoidart, where Donald now was, pressingly desiring him to come to meet the Prince at Borrodale. Donald immediately set out, and, in passing through the forest of Glenbiasdale, he encountered a stranger walking by himself, who, on approaching, asked if he was Donald Macleod of Galtrigal?

Donald, instantly recognising him despite his ragged clothing, said, 'I am the same man, please your Highness; at your service.' 'Then,' said the Prince, 'you see, Donald, I am in distress; I therefore throw myself into your bosom, and let you do with me what you like. I hear you are an honest man, and fit to be trusted.'

The Prince then proposed that Donald should go with letters from him to Sir Alexander Macdonald at Monkstadt, and to Macleod of Dunvegan, soliciting their protection. Donald stared his Royal Highness in the face, and said, 'Is your Royal Highness in earnest in making such a mad request? The chiefs mentioned, you must be aware, are your enemies, and are at this moment employed in searching for you in the Isles and elsewhere.'

'Well, well, Donald,' said the Prince, 'all things seem to be adverse to me, but my good friend, you must at all events pilot me, and that immediately, to the Long Island.' Donald at once replied that he was ready to be of any service in his power, and risk his very life in his behalf — but that he wouldn't take the messages.

In order to put the Prince's plan into execution with all possible speed, the most expert seamen and the most substantial boat in the place were obtained and equipped at Borrodale, in the bay of Loch-nan-uagh, near the spot where the Prince first landed at on his arrival in Scotland. The office of Captain was delegated to Donald of Galtrigal.

On the evening of April 26 the Prince, O'Neil, O'Sullivan and others, seated themselves in the boat, but Donald Macleod did not want to set sail because experience told him that a storm was about to break. Charles however refused his advice to stay in port for the night.

In less than an hour, a terrible storm arose, with thunder and lightning; and the crew had more than enough to do to keep the boat from swamping. The crested waves rose around like dark rolling mountains, and, breaking into the frail vessel in gushing streams, gave the crew very hard work to bale them out. Rain fell in torrents, and the brooding darkness like a gloomy curtain of death, was momentarily illuminated by the bright flashes of lightning that darted from cloud to cloud!

They had no compass, no chart, and scarcely any hope of safety. They could avoid neither rock, nor island, nor shore, nor quicksand; but were compelled to dash on before a sweeping Easterly hurricane, and trust to Providence.

The Prince, greatly impressed with the danger, frequently addressed the pilot, and said, 'Oh! Donald, Donald, I fear that all is over with us; this is worse than Culloden by far.' Donald replied, that while they were afloat there was hope, and that He who had the winds and waves under His command, was able to preserve them if they placed confidence in Him.

Such was the case, for at daybreak, much to their surprise and their great joy, they saw the hills of the Long Island straight ahead, and in less than an hour after they landed in a creek at Rossinish, on the east side of Benbecula, where with great difficulty they secured the boat, and their lives. The natives observing their approach, immediately assembled, and took them to a place of safety.

But back on the mainland supporters of Charles were paying a terrible price.

Men, women, and children, were murdered in cold blood, and mercy was extended to none. Those who were not massacred were banished from the smoking ashes of their burning dwellings.

Thus cruelly pursued, they had no alternative but to die of cold and hunger on the moors, or to perish in mountain recesses and in the caves of the rocks.

The rebel chiefs were doomed by the Royalists, as far as possible, to the same fate. The castles and strongholds of Cluny, Keppoch, Glengyle, Glengarry, Lochiel, and many others, were plundered and burnt to the ground. The devastations committed by the English army were a stain on humanity.

Meanwhile Prince Charles had begun his wanderings in the Western Isles, where he ran many hair-breadth esacpes for his life.

His whereabouts were always known to some one or other of

EAN DONAN CASTLE, WESTER ROSS

LEAKIN, ISLE OF SKYE

DUNVEGAN CASTLE.

CULLODEN

PEACEFUL SCENE ON UIST

G, SKYE

THE GRAVES OF FLORA AND HER HUSBAND ALLAN at Kilmuir, Isle of Skye, stand side by side

his faithful adherents. His wellwishers in the place were numerous, and of considerable influence.

Among them were the influential clan chief Clanranald and his brother Boisdale, Banker Macdonald, Mr O'Sullivan, Mr O'Neil, the Macdonalds of Baileshear, and his own 'fidus Achates', Donald Macleod of Galtrigal. Clanranald and his excellent wife had selected twelve trusty men, whom they had sworn to fidelity, as messengers and guides to his Royal Highness on every emergency when their services were required.

At last the danger became so imminent that the Prince's friends held a consultation at Ormiclade, the residence of Clanranald, where it was agreed that an attempt should be made to effect his rescue through a young lady in the neighbourhood, Miss Flora Macdonald.

This family Macdonald

Flora was the daughter of Ranald Macdonald, younger of Milton, in South Uist. She was born in 1722, which made her two years younger than the Prince.

Flora's mother was Marion, daughter of the Rev Angus Macdonald, for some years Parish minister of the Island of Gigha. This clergyman was noted in the country as a man of extraordinary muscular strength. He had no equal for any athletic exercises requiring great bodily power.

He was a mild, generous, and much respected gentleman. The natives of the Hebrides were always noted for their attention and kindness to strangers, but the Rev Angus Macdonald was proverbial for his genuine Highland hospitality.

His wife was a talented and accomplished lady, a daughter of Macdonald of Largie, in Kintyre.

Flora was the only daughter of the family, but she had two brothers. The elder, Ranald, was a very promising youth, who appeared to inherit his reverend grandfather's activity and strength.

Flora's younger brother, Angus, succeeded his father at Milton, while her mother, in 1728, married, as her second husband, Hugh Macdonald of Armadale in Skye, a Captain of Militia in the Long Island during the Prince's wanderings there.

As we shall see later, had it not been for the friendly disposition of Hugh Macdonald towards the Prince, in all probability his Royal Highness could never have escaped from the Long Island.

When Flora's mother, after her marriage, was about to move to her new home in Skye, she naturally wanted to take her little and only daughter along with her, but her son, Angus, was reluctant to part with his sister. She was only two years of age when she lost her father, and six at the date of her mother's second marriage.

The mother and son could not agree at all about the little girl. Eventually it was decided to let Flora choose for herself. She replied: 'I will stay at Milton because I love it. I do not know Skye, and do not care for it. I will therefore remain with Angus until my dear mamma comes back for me.'

Flora was a most interesting child, wise beyond her years, and more sage in her remarks than her contemporaries. There were no children in the family at Milton and she grew up almost exclusively in adult company.

But in addditon to all this, she was naturally a precocious little girl, who showed an early taste for the beautiful, great, and grand in nature. She had been known to stand for hours admiring the battling of the elements, when the bold Atlantic rose in mountains of foam.

It was a magnificent sight to behold the storm in its fury dashing on the western shores of the Island, and showering its briny spray over the length and the breadth of the land. The whole scenery of the place, with the grandeur of the surrounding isles, could never fail to rouse feelings of admiration in the minds of young or old.

Being an only daughter, and left fatherless at so early an age, created no doubt a general feeling of sympathy in Flora's favour. All this, together with her agreeable behaviour, caused her name to be generally brought forward, as an example, by parents in correcting their children, asking them, 'When will you resemble Flora of Milton?'

She was naturally smart, clever, and active, but cautious in her movements, and was invariably the principal or leader in every game, or juvenile frolic in which she engaged.

She became a particular favourite with all the respectable families in the Island, especially with Clanranald and his lady, his brother Boisdale and family, and her own relatives at Baileshear. Lady Clanranald was more like a mother than a distant relative.

When she was about thirteen years of age, Lady Clanranald insisted on her remaining at Ormiclade, that she might get the benefit of instruction from a governess who had been provided by Clanranald for his own children. And for about three years her home was in the hospitable mansion of Clanranald, with the exception of occasional short trips to Skye, to visit her mother at Armadale.

She by far excelled in her lessons the daughters of the family, and they became jealous of poor Flora, hinting that the governess was more attentive to her than to them.

In 1739 Lady Margaret Macdonald, of Monkstadt, Skye, wife of Sir Alexander of the Isles, wrote to Lady Clanranald, requesting a visit from Flora whom she had not seen for two years. Lady Margaret felt a deep interest in Flora's welfare, and she was much pleased with her prudence, general conduct, and amiable disposition.

Flora goes to Edinburgh

She and Sir Alexander had arranged to pass the winter in Edinburgh, and they wanted Flora to accompany them and finish her education there. Flora gratefully accepted.

It was proposed by Lady Margaret that Flora should visit the capital during the autumn, but circumstances occurred to prevent this. Lady Clanranald was an invalid at the time, as was also Flora's brother Angus, at Milton, in both cases from neglected colds.

Flora's kind, generous heart would not permit her to leave these friends in a state of convalescence; this proved most fortunate as the sloop by which she proposed to sail was wrecked en route to Edinburgh, and not a single life was saved.

Fortunately, in course of time her invalid friends recovered, and Flora stayed at Ormiclade and Milton during the winter and spring. Early in the following summer (1740) she embraced another opportunity of visiting her friends in Skye.

Throughout that island she was welcomed by every family of respectability, but particularly so by those at Scorribreck, Kingsburgh, Cuiderach, and Monkstadt. Arrangements were now made for her departure to Edinburgh during the ensuing months of September or October, according to the state of the weather.

About the beginning of August, Flora bade farewell to her friends in Skye, and revisited her native Isle, which was the most dear to her Highland heart. Towards the end of September, she took her passage from Uist to Glasgow in a small schooner laden with cured cod and ling for the southern markets.

The captain was Roderick Macdonald, a native of Moidart, on the mainland. Rory was a very jolly, middle-aged tar, who materially diminished the tediousness of the passage by his singing of Gaelic songs, in which he could not easily be excelled.

In this respect he met with a very congenial spirit in his only cabin passenger, Flora being one who greatly admired the Celtic muse of her skipper.

At length, after an ordinary passage, the schooner arrived safely at the Broomielaw, Glasgow. Two days later Flora found her way by some public conveyance to Edinburgh.

On her arrival she went straight to a boarding-school provided for her through the kind services of Lady Margaret. This Ladies' Seminary, which was attended by about half-a-dozen, was taught by a Miss Henderson, in the Old Stamp-Office Close, High Street.

During Flora's stay in Edinburgh, which lasted for over three years, she had the good fortune to be introduced to many familes of high rank and distinction. She invariably conducted herself with such a degree of unassuming modesty as added materially to her appreciation in the eyes of others.

Flora attended closely to her education. She considerably excelled her fellow pupils in the comparatively few branches of education in which instruction was given to females at that period.

In the musical department, a sort of small harp was the instrument generally used for inculcating a knowledge of that interesting science. Flora, however, preferred practising on a spinet or small pianoforte, at which she was able to play a great variety of Highland airs and 'piobairachds' with a degree of grace and ease that delighted all around her. She was also gifted with a sweet, mellow voice and sang Gaelic songs exceedingly well, much to the gratification and amusement of the company present.

She was frequently asked to sing in the drawing-rooms of the noble and great, where no one present understood a single vocable of the stanzas she so sweetly sang.

Having passed nearly three seasons with the ladies in the Old Stamp-Office Close, she afterwards lived mainly in the house of Lady Margaret and Sir Alexander.

Flora became so thoroughly domesticated and useful to her ladyship that she was persuaded to stay in Edinburgh for more than a year after she had made up her mind to return to her mother, and her friends in the Long Island. Sir Alexander was not at that time in very robust health; and, by the advice of his medical attendants, he remained for two years in Edinburgh without returning to Skye.

News of the disastrous defeat of the British forces at Fontenoy reached Edinburgh and caused alarm. In a few weeks rumours were prevalent that the victory gained by the French over the allied forces of Britain was hailed as a propitious event for the prospects of the young Chevalier and his numerous partisans.

Flora and family hear rumours of Rebellion

As the days were passing, these rumours gained credence in the eyes of the community at large. The well-known intrigues of the youthful aspirant to the British throne were the continual subject of conversation among the citizens of all classes.

Sir Alexander Macdonald had much at stake, and should a revolution be attempted, his position was a critical one. He had to stand true to his King and country and it was important he returned to Skye.

Flora was at the time on a visit to her kind friend Bishop Forbes at Leith, and a messenger was sent requesting her to return to Edinburgh without delay. Sir Alexander and his lady were making ready for the journey home, and she was to accompany them.

On June 3, the whole party went on board the 'Brothers' in Leith Harbour, and set sail on the evening of the same day. They arrived at Inverness eight days later.

Sir Alexander, before leaving Edinburgh, had written to his servants in Skye to send three horses properly saddled to the Highland capital, to take Lady Margaret, Miiss Flora, and himself to the island. At that time there were no public roads, but rough riding paths from Inverness to Skye, making the journey very tiring and uncomfortable, especially for ladies.

Sir Alexander and his party passed a whole week very pleasantly at Inverness, and were visited during their stay by most of the surrounding lairds.

Two days after, three saddled horses arrived in town to take them home. Each horse had his *'Gille- ceann-srein'*, or attendant, who walked on the right side of the horse to protect the rider.

The party on leaving Inverness by the rough mountainous path by Kimmylies and through Caiplich, Abriachan, and Glen-Urquhart, arrived safely that evening at Invermoriston House, where they remained for two days enjoying the chief's hospitality with a select company of guests.

The next route was by Cluany and Glenshiel. At the latter place, on account of a heavy rainfall, by which the mountain rivulets were swollen into impassable streams, they had to pass the night in a small inn, where they received all the comforts that the little Highland hostelry could afford.

Starting early the following morning, they went through Kintail, crossed Kyleakin ferry into Skye, and arrived late in the evening at the hospitable house of Corriechatachain, where the Mackinnon of the day gladly welcomed his unexpected guests.

Miss Flora was more than delighted to find her mother at Corriechatachain. She had come from her own residence at Armadale, a distance of about twenty miles, to welcome her daughter back to Skye after so long an absence.

Two days later Sir Alexander and his party, with their retinue arrived safely at Monkstadt.

The Prince lands in Scotland

Flora Macdonald was gifted with the rare capacity of adapting herself to any circumstances by which she was surrounded, or any events that might befall her.

She was a dutiful daughter, an affectionate wife, a prudent mother, an unchangeable friend, an amiable companion, and a sincere Christian. By those that knew her best, she was appreciated most, and perhaps by none more than Sir Alexander Macdonald of the Isles, and his talented lady, who treated her is if she had been their own child.

After such a long absence from her native Isle, she appeared most anxious to get a passage there to once again see her brother at Milton and her friends at Ormiclade. On the last day of June, after remaining four days at Monkstadt, she secured a passage in a small sloop bound for Benbecula, where she landed in safety that evening.

Her reception by Lady Clanranald was a most cordial one,and her arrival was heartily greeted by a numerous circle of relatives and friends.

Poor Flora was quite bewildered by the reception and the many expressions of congratulation. Old Clanranald himself seemed extremely happy and declared :— 'Flora, my dear, I rejoice to see your comely face again. You are welcome back to the Isle of your birth, for the household was devoid of joy and gladness since you left it; and even 'Coelag' itself (the small pianoforte), as if under lamentation, was mute.'

At that time the excitement that spread through the whole Island, like most other parts of Scotland, was very great, because of the rumours that the Young Chevalier was soon to visit them. The partisans of His Royal Highness from these quarters, who were along with him in France, especially Banker Macdonald, Kinlochmoidart's brother, kept regular contact with their friends in the Isles and on the mainland about the movements of the Prince.

The consequences were, that the different chiefs, and the most intelligent of their supporters, were unsure how they ought to act when the crisis came to pass. Continued meetings were held and the claims of the Prince to the throne of his forefathers were freely discussed, but were as freely condemned by some as they were aprroved by others.

In this respect acrimonious differences arose betwixt chief and chief, brother and brother, father and son; the Highlands were truly divided.

It was expected by friends of the Prince, as well as by himself, that the powerful chiefs, Sir Alexander Macdonald, and Macleod of Dunvegan, who could have raised more than a thousand men each, would have at once joined his Royal Highness, but both declined. It can scarcely be said that the conduct of these chiefs was strictly honourable, as they promised their allegiance to the cause of the Prince, on condition that he brought along with him a sufficient number of men and money, and munitions of war; but seeing that he failed in this, they considered themselves released from their engagement, and at once refused their aid.

Against this background the news spread rapidly that the Doutelle, with the Prince on board, had arrived at the Island of Erriska, in the Sound of Barra, on the 23rd day of July, 1745.

Soon after casting anchor, the Prince and most of his party landed on the Island, and were taken to the house of Angus Macdonald, tacksman of Erriska, where they spent the night. After the fatigues of eighteen days at sea they were all very tired.

As the Prince did not at the time reveal himself, his hospitable landlord took him to be a chief attendant on the gentleman who had just landed from the frigate. Unfortunately the house was so infested with smoke from the large peat fire in the middle of the chamber that the Prince frisked about, and frequently went outside the door for fresh air.

The landlord was surprised, and perhaps a little offended at the stranger's restlessness, so that he called out, with rather an indignant smile, 'Plague take that fellow! What is wrong with him, that he can neither sit nor stand still — neither can he keep within doors nor without doors.'

The Prince, eager to lose as little time as possible, made enquiries about old Clanranald, and other influential parties in the adjacent islands. He was told that Clanranald was at home at Ormiclade; that his brother Alexander was at Boisdale; and that young Clanranald was on the mainland at Moidart.

He was aware that the Clanranald branch of the Macdonalds was always favourable to the cause of the Stuarts, and consequently he sent a messenger to Boisdale seeking an interview with him, to secure the support of the clan at large, especially that of his brother the laird, and of his nephew, young Clanranald.

Boisdale appeared next morning on board the frigate; the interview took place, and it was anything bu agreeable. The conversation with the Prince was firm and determined, and in all respects more plain than pleasant.

Boisdale told the Prince that he made up his mind to advise his brother and nephew not to get involved in such a hopeless and dangerous enterprise. He further stated that Sir Alexander Macdonald and Macleod of Macleod were determined to stand aloof, and that under these circumstances, his best advice to his Royal Highness was to return at once to France, and forget forever such a foolish undertaking.

The Prince was furious at this, but he restrained his feelings, and appeared amiable and very agreeable.

Next day the Doutelle arrived safely at the bay of Loch nan Uagh, between Arisaig and Moidart. The Prince, bitterly disappointed at the coldness and indifference of Boisdale in not backing his cause, sent a letter at once to young Clanranald by Banker Macdonald, that his brother Kinlochmoidart might accompany young Clanranald on board.

They were cheerfully welcomed by the Prince, but in course of conversation young Clanranald enlarged upon the hopelessness of the adventure, and the improbability of success, and was, in short, like his uncle Boisdale, against taking part. Charles, seeing that young Clanranald greatly sympathised with him, and seemed to be warlmy interested in his case, used all the powers of his eloquence to persuade him to take part and eventually won his backing.

The Prince was as yet hopeful, despite Boisdale's declaration, that Sir Alexander Macdonald and Macleod of Macleod would join him with their forces. Accordingly, he despatched young Clanranald and Mr Allan Macdonald, a brother of Kinlochmoidart, to these chiefs with letters, earnestly seeking their aid.

Both chiefs replied to the message of his Royal Highness, that they considered his cause a desperate one, and that they would not engage in it.

The history of the Rebellion of 1745 is already well known, ending, as already stated, in the disastrous defeat at Culloden.

When viewed in its varied features it may be considered to rank high among the achievements of ancient and modern times. The interests at stake were of the highest importance not only to the Royal adventurer himself, but likewise to the different clans and septs that so imprudently espoused his cause.

What could be more hazardous than to rush beyond the middle of England, and to cross a hostile country to the heart of London itself?

As the talented Chambers has so well expressed it, 'the expedition was done in the face of two armies, each capable of utterly annihilating it; and the weather was such as to add a thousand personal miseries to the general evils of the campaign.

'A magnaminity was preserved even in retreat, beyond that of ordinary soldiers, and instead of flying in wild disorder, a prey to their pursuers, these desultory bands had turned against and smitten the superior army of the enemy with a rigour which effectually checked it. They had carried the standard of Glenfinnan a hundred and fifty miles into a country full of foes, and now they brought it back unscathed through the accumulated dangers of storm and war.'

While the clans and country gentlemen — chieftains and their vassals — Dukes and Lords — and all ranks and classes in the Highlands and Lowlands, and over Scotland at large, viewed the Rebellion with the deepest anxiety, Miss Flora Macdonald experienced her own share of the general calamity. Personally she adhered to the loyal principles and feelings of her chief, Sir Alexander Macdonald, as well as of Old Clanranald and his brother Boisdale.

On the other hand, her amiable disposition in a sense compelled her to sympathise with the unfortunate Prince under all his hardships and sufferings. She kept up a close correspondence with old friends and acquaintanes in Edinburgh and elsewhere, and thereby became fully informed as to the various movements of Charles.

The family at Ormiclade, with whom Flora principally resided, were deeply affected. Old Clanranald was distressed by the part which his son had taken in embracing the Royal adventurer's cause.

So was Lady Clanranald but Flora soothed them in their grief. She assured tham that they would be spared to see all going well.

In due time the result of the battle of Culloden became known in the Long Island, and created mixed feelings in the minds of the chief men of the place. To some the news afforded no ordinary pleasure, while to others it created unbounded terror, under the dread that the ruling and now successful dynasty might inflict vengeance, and even the penalty of death, on those who had supported the Royal adventurer's cause.

By this time some of Charles' movements became known to the Government officials,and immmediate steps were taken to secure his arrest, dead or alive.

The news of his arrival created unprecedented commotion all over the Long Island. By this time it became well known that 'rebel hunting', as Cumberland and his lawless soldiery called it, was mercilessly practised in every quarter.

It was too well known that the Duke had issued a proclamation warning of immmediate death, by being shot or hanged, against all persons who harboured any of the rebels, or aided them to escape.

Already about two thousand regular troops and militia-men were posted in suitable localities all over the island. Every avenue was guarded, every ferry had its watch, and every highway and hill-road was protected by soldiers.

The lochs and bays, and the sea-coast all around, were so studded with sloops of war and cutters of all sizes, that no craft could possibly leave the island or come to it unknown, except perhaps, under cover of darkness. No two individuals could talk together on the highway without arousing the suspicion of some of the watching military.

The only consolation for the Prince was the fact that he had many sincere friends on the island, who were ready to strain every nerve for his safety.

Besides the friends who a companied him from France, he had Clanranald, the proprietor of the island, Macdonald of Boisdale, the Macdonalds of Baileshear, and almost all the ladies of the island. Whether loyal or Jacobite, all were united in the wish that the Royal fugitive would escape with his life.

Lady Clanranald and Miss Flora were continually engaged

devising schemes for the protection and release of the Prince, whom as yet they had never seen.

Twelve powerful and trustworthy men, who could acquit themselves by sea or land, were selcted by Lady Clanranald to be in readiness by night and day, should their services be required. Flora very frequently talked with these gallant islanders about the risky duties they might be called upon to perform.

One morning as two of them had come to Ormiclade to tell how he had passed the night in a rocky cave, Flora met them at the door and asked them, 'Is he nice? Is he cheerful? Is he at all humble and pleasant?'

On another occasion she began, for her own amusement, to taunt them in a jocular manner, by telling them how to become far wealthier than Clanranald in less than a day's time. 'Oh! tell us, do tell us, how that can come to pass. More wealthy than our noble chief! Can such really be the case?'

'Oh yes, perfectly true' said Flora with a smile, 'and I will now tell you what means you are to use. Go immediately and give up the Prince to my step-father, Captain Hugh Macdonald, and as sure as the sun is now shining in the firmament, you shall have fifteen thousand pounds a-piece for your great loyalty in doing so.'

The answer was short, but decisive — 'Goodness forbid! Alas! should we receive the world around which the sun revolves, we would never betray our Royal youth.'

Neither would they, nor any other Highlander then living.

Clanranald, Boisdale, and their namesakes at Baileshear, with Lady Clanranald and Miss Flora, held a private council at Ormiclade, as to what must be done, quickly as every hour increased the danger to their unfortunate Prince. It was resolved that he should be transported to Stornoway, as he might there receive the chance of a vessel to France.

They set sail for Stornoway

Donald Macleod of Galtrigal, the Prince's faithful friend and pilot, was sent for, and all the plans were explained to him. Despite the obvious danger, he agreed to execute his part of the scheme, if provided with a crew selected by hismelf. It would include his own son, Murdoch.

Before the battle of Culloden was fought, Murdoch was attending the Grammar School of, Inverness, being then a youth of sixteen or seventeen. He understood that the battle was to be fought on a certain day, and on the morning of that day he left his school, procured a sword and a dirk, and made for the battlefield.

He stood there and fought for the Prince, and came through the fighting unscathed.

Seeing that longer delay was dangerous, the party set sail for Stornoway on April 29, and Donald Macleod, knowing the course well, took his place at the helm.

They had no sooner gone to sea, about midnight, than a severe storm arose, which, owing to the darkness of the night, placed them in danger, not only of being swamped, but of being dashed against the rocks or jutting headlands. The crew, however, bravely held on, under the direction of Donald, while two of them by turns kept constantly baling the boat, to prevent it from filling.

About dawn they took shelter in a creek in the small Island of Glass, on the coast of Harris. The tacksman of the island, Donald Campbell, to whom alone they made themselves known, treated them very kindly, and suggested that the Prince should remain with him, while Macleod should visit Stornoway, to secure, if possible, a vessel to take the Royal fugitive to France.

This plan was agreed upon, and after Macleod had reached the capital of the Lews, he thought that all would be well as he had secured a vessel for the intended purpose. His next step was to send a messenger immediately for the Prince to the

Island of Glass, as no time was to be lost.

As the storm had not abated, sailing was impossible, and the Royal fugitive had to walk through the trackless wilds of the Lews to the vicinity of Stornoway.

Unfortunately one of Donald's crew got the worse of drink, and told his associates by way of boast that the hired vessel was intended to convey Prince Charles to France. This created considerable alarm in the town, and it was decided that no vessel would be given on any conditions whatever, as such a move might involve the natives in serious trouble.

So the Prince and his associates then sailed back to Benbecula, to trust once more to the schemes and contrivances of his friends there.

During his stay near Stornoway, the Prince received shelter, and was entertained at the house of Mrs Mackenzie of Kildun at Arinish, about a mile from the village. Here his Royal Highness and friends spent many anxious hours devising escape schemes, while they waited on the stormy sea to calm.

Some of them, dreading immediate danger, proposed to hide in the hills, but the Prince objected. He suggested, if they did not make their way to Benbecula, that they should attempt to return to the mainland, in the hope of meeting with some vessel from France.

Donald Macleod and the whole party, however, refused to entertain this hazardous plan, as their craft was too small, the voyage too long, and the danger of meeting with Government vessels very great. It was then agreed that they would leave Arinish before daybreak, and proceed southward along the coast of the Long Island.

The morning was wet and somewhat stormy, but the wind was favourable, and they sailed along with great speed.

At length they observed two ships against the horizon, evidently approaching them, and to avoid the danger of meeting them, they entered a creek in the small Island of Iffurt, a little north of the Island of Glass. Iffurt was occupied by a few fishermen, who, on observing the party, took them to be press-boat men, or a press-gang from some warship, and they consequently took to their heels at once, and hid among the rocks.

Owing to the continued storm and other dangers, Charles and his friends remained four days on this island. Next morning after their arrival they discovered the terrified fishermen, and assured them that they were quite safe.

The poor men were overjoyed, and in return did everything in their power to show kindness to the strangers. They had plenty of fish and fuel, but their dwelling was a miserable hut, over which the Prince's party spread the mainsail of their boat to exclude the rain.

On May 10 they left Iffurt and sailed for Glass. Finding, to their great disappointment, that their friend Donald Campbell had fled under dread of being seized for entertaining the Prince, they did not linger. Instead, they steered their course southward along the coast of Harris.

While crossing the mouth of Finsbay, they were observed by Captain Ferguson's warship which lay at the time in the bay. A well-manned boat was despatched in pursuit, but fortunately the fugitives escaped, having concealed themselves, in a small creek near Rodill, in Harris.

Shipwrecked!

At nightfall they left their hiding-place, and sailed along the coast of North Uist, but when near Lochmaddy, another warship spotted them, and immediately gave chase. Fortunately the Prince and his companions reached Benbecula, and just as they were getting ashore, the increasing storm, blowing off the land, drove the vessel of the enemy out to sea.

To avoid seizure by the man-of-war, which was close in pursuit, they dashed their boat, under full sail, into a narrow creek, where the frail bark was splintered to fragments against the jutting rocks, leaving the Prince and his companions floundering amid the foaming waves.

They all however managed to reach dry land, whilst Charles cheerfully remarked to his friends that his escapes were marvellous, and that he believed in his heart that a kind

Providence would permit him to be rescued in the end.

It has often been said that 'truth is stranger than fiction.' This adage is perhaps in no instance more strikingly verified than in the case of the unfortunate Prince. His varied adventures, his critical dangers, his at times hopeful prospects, and his frequent hair-breadth escapes, are incidents in his daring career for which it is difficult to find a parallel in the history of any other man.

One thing, however, is certain, that the cause of his having been rescued in the end arose not so much from any prudence or precaution on his part as from friendly feelings secretly cherished by some of those employed by the Government to arrest him.

It is well known that great sympathy was felt for 'Bonnie Prince Charlie', even by office-bearers of the Crown, all over the Highlands and Islands. Indeed on several occasions they might easily have arrested him during his perilous wanderings in the Long Island if they had had a mind to do so.

It is true, on the other hand, that the captains and commanders of the frigates and sloops of war which scoured the creeks and coasts of the Western Isles were all determined to capture him dead or alive. These however were generally confined to their own vessels at sea, and were consequently at considerable disadvantage in seizing their prey, who avoided going to sea, unless compelled by necessity.

In his perilous adventures from Stornoway to Benbecula he had to combat, not only with the violence of the elements, but likewise against the perpetual dread of being seized at any moment by some of the emissaries of the fleet of Government vessels that sailed all around to capture him.

On his arrival at Benbecula he and his faithful companions resorted, under the cover of night, to a small hut or hovel that lay at a little distance, where they attempted to boil some shell-fish which they found among the rocks where they landed.

Next morning at daybreak the Prince sent Donald Macleod to acquaint Clanranald of his arrival at Benbecula, and of the dangers by which he was beset. Donald told the chief all the difficulties they had encountered in their fruitless voyage to Stornoway.

Clanranald was deeply concerned with Donald's account of matters, thinking that by that time his Royal Highness had been safely transported to France. The worthy chief was sorely perplexed, and as he paced up and down the room he addressed the faithful Donald: 'Alas! alas! Donald, I am greatly afraid that the sun of Charles, which was at one time so brilliant, is about soon to sink in blood and in darkness.'

All this time Lady Clanranald sat silently in her armchair, sobbing and shedding tears. Flora was also present but appeared spirited and cheerful.

Turning round to Clanranald she declared: 'I am astonished at your expressions to Donald, for while there is life there is hope. Remember that ever Blessed Being who planted in the firmament of heaven yon sun which now shines so brightly is all-powerful to rescue Charles from the snares of his enemies.' Clanranald could not help smiling at his amiable protegee's confident remarks, and said, 'Oh! my dear·Flora, you have never lost your courage, and I hope you never shall.'

The interview ended by Clanranald sending the Prince a message via Donald that he would visit him in his hiding-place without delay.

After Donald's departure the chief became very impatient, and resolved to set off the same afternoon. In order not to appear at a distance from home without some apparent purpose, he equipped himself with all his shooting accoutrements, his gun, lead-belt and powder flask, and started through the hills to the hiding place.

At the same time Niel MacEachainn, who generally resided at Ormiclade, was to resort that same evening to the Prince's hovel, with a supply of shirts, shoes and stockings, and a quantity of brandy and wine, to contribute to the scanty comforts of his Royal Highness. Niel MacEachainn (Niel, the son of Hector Macdonald) was a faithful inmate at Ormiclade, being an intelligent, smart Jack-of-all-trades.

He was a handsome well educated youth and made himself generally useful about the place. He had spent several years in

Paris, where he had been taken when a mere boy by Banker Macdonald as body-servant. He learned to speak the French language fluently, and was therefore a very suitable messenger to send to the Prince, as he could talk in that language to his Royal Highness unintelligibly to all around him.

When Clanranald arrived at the Prince's hovel he was shocked at its miserable state, and he persuaded Charles to move to a more comfortable retreat in the hill of Corrodale.

Meantime the Prince falling short of means, despatched his trusty friend Donald Macleod, with letters to General Murray, and Lochiel, craving a supply of money without delay. Macleod accidentally met these gentlemen at the head of Loch Arkaig, in Lochaber, where they gave him a written reply to the Prince expressing regret that they had no money to send him.

The new residence of the fugitive was the Forest-house of Glen-corrodale, and although it was in a very lonely, sequestered place, he found it more comfortable and suitable than his last abode.

It was dismally gloomy, and deeply buried in the Corrodale hills, yet it had one great advantage in that its situation afforded recreation. The forest abounded in game of all kinds, grouse and deer, and the Prince possessed great dexterity in the use of his gun.

But he used it at times very incautiously. One afternoon, he and two of his faithful followers went to the moor, expecting to shoot a roe or a deer.

Turning a blind eye

After the Prince had fired at some grouse he observed, to his horror, a small band of militia on the shoulder of the nearby hill. He had no alternative but to run and conceal himself in a ravine close by, and give his gun to one of his attendants, with instructions to go forward in the direction of the soldiers, and should they meet them, appear as if nothing were amiss.

It was later discovered that the militia was commanded by Captain Hugh Macdonald, Flora's step-father, who was at the time well aware that the Prince was one of the shooting party.

But, being a Jacobite at heart, Hugh had no desire to capture the Prince.

On several other occasions Charles had very narrow escapes from the troops of militia in the island and as day after day passed, matters were becoming more critical and dangerous.

The Government authorities became aware that he was unquestionably in South Uist or Benbecula, and they issued strict orders to surround these islands with sloops of war, and carefully to guard every creek, loch, and bay, to prevent any possibility of escape.

Besides these guardian vessels, additional companies of militia and regular soldiers were landed in the Long Island, to search hills and dales, and to prevent any sailing craft of any size to go to sea until they had searched and ransacked, not only the crews individually, but all their bunkers and recesses. All this was done to prevent the concealment of papers or letters going to friends in any quarter that might suggest plans for effecting the rescue of the Prince.

Lady Margaret in Skye became fully aware of the measures taken; but her ladyship was doubtful whether the Prince himself had been apprised of the real danger, so she sent a verbal communication to Baileshear, by the master of a sloop sailing for Benbecula, pressing upon him to see the Prince, and to make everything known to him.

As soon as opportunity offered, Baileshear, with his friend Boisdale, went at night to Glen-corrodale and briefed him. Charles, grateful to Lady Margaret for her interest, wrote a kind letter of thanks, which he handed to Baileshear for delivery.

Baileshear at the same time told him that the master of the sloop who conveyed Lady Margaret's message was returning to Skye in a day or two with a number of young cattle, and that he would send the letter by him.

To avoid detection Baileshear enclosed it in one from himself to his brother Captain Donald Roy Macdonald, who resided at the time with Sir Alexander Macdonald, at Monkstadt. Captain Macdonald was lame in consequence of a musket ball having gone through his left foot at Culloden.

Baileshear gave strict instructions to his brother to see that his own letter and that of the Prince to Lady Margaret were consigned to the flames when read. This was done to the great regret of her ladyship afterwards.

Baileshear pointed out in his letter that the Prince would require to leave the Long Island without delay, and would probably be landed on the small Island of Fladda-chuain, on the north coast of Troternish; but this was not the case.

Baileshear was much perplexed as to how he would secure the letters from the searching of the harpies who were sure to ransack every hole and corner of the cattle-ship. A little before that time a vessel had been wrecked on the coast of South Uist, which had been laden with a mixed cargo; and among other things several casks of coffee beans had drifted ashore and were sold for trifling prices to the natives.

Baileshear filled one of these small barrels with beans and placed his letter in the bottom of the cask. He then covered the whole with a suitable lid, and addressed it to his brother in Skye. The Captain was instructed to tell in delivering the cask, where the letter would be found.

This done, the craft was ready to set sail, but no sooner had the Government officials observed that preparations were being made for departing than they went on board and searched the crew and all the keeping-places in the vessel. Even the lid of the barrel which contained the letter was lifted, when they found it full to the brim with beans of coffee.

All was found well and they leapt ashore.

A new hiding place

A few days after this the Prince came to understand that Boisdale and his own faithful adherent, Donald Macleod of Galtrigal, were taken prisoners, and this sadly grieved him. Dreading that his quarters at Glen-corrodale had been made known to the Government spies, he left the place under cover of night with Captain O'Neil, and went to a more concealed retreat in Benbecula.

By this time the whole country was in a state of great

excitement and alarm. Night after night Ormiclade was crowded with the friends of the Prince, in order to devise some plan for his escape.

Clanranald did not think his present place of concealment at all safe, hence the necessity of having him removed at once from his hut, and getting him into some natural cave still more difficult of access, until he might be conveyed from the island.

Captain O'Neil, the faithful companion and friend of the Prince, along with Baileshear and others, waited one evening upon the laird, at Ormiclade, for the purpose of adopting a rescue scheme for Charles. Several plans were proposed, but each had some insurmountable difficulty.

At length Lady Clanranald addressed herself to Flora Macdonald, who sat silently and pensively in a corner of the room. 'Flora, dear', said her ladyship, 'just consider for a moment the dignity, the honour, the glory, of saving the life of your lawful Prince!'

'My dear lady', responded Flora, 'the matter is difficult, perplexing, and dangerous, and it might be ruinous to all to plunge into any scheme without pondering over it in all its bearings.'

'All true, my dear Flora, but we all know that you are the only person, in this trying emergency, whom we deem at all likely to be able to effect the rescue, if you have the moral courage to attempt it.'

'Moral courage!' retorted Flora, as if hurt by the reflection. 'Moral courage! Ah! yes, my dear Lady Clanranald, moral courage will never fail me, never; yet still moral courage may not be able to work impossibilities. I care not to endanger, or even sacrifice my valueless life, if I can but see my way to save the valuable life of the unfortunate Prince. As yet, however, the prospects are to me dark and gloomy.'

It was a moment of great suspense to every member of the friendly circle on that eventful evening at Orimclade, but not so much to any as to the gallant Flora. She was blessed with a sound, discriminating judgment, which braced her to discharge what she considered important duties.

It was now, however, that the young heroine was put to the test. She had to decide at once against the influence of three conflicting elements, all important in themselves.

She had to brave the danger of the doubtful enterprise. She had to run the risk of entailing ruin and disgrace upon her chief, Sir Alexander Macdonald, and his Lady, and she had to meet the strong and perhaps reasonable objections to her hazardous undertaking by her only living brother, whom she dearly loved.

Dilemma for Flora

No doubt poor Flora was at the moment in a very perplexing dilemma. Those around her placed all confidence in her, as a smart, intelligent young woman of excellent address and prudence; and they encouraged her by the assurance that her step-father, Captain Hugh Macdonald, who then commanded a detachment of the Militia, and who retained a warm feeling at heart towards the Stuarts, would at once procure for her a passport under his own hand to enable her to leave the Long Island.

Flora listened calmly to all these remarks, and for some time made no reply. Lady Clanranald again pressed her for a decision.

'Indeed, my dear Lady' answered Flora, 'I have come to the conclusion that the chances of success are extremely small. I am really of the opinion that the escape of the Prince to Skye is almost impossible, and I will state my reasons.

'You know well, my dear Lady, that the Macdonald, Macleod and Campbell militia are just now commanding every pass and creek. Then it is certain that the Prince is well known to all these to be on this island. It is publicly announced that thirty thousand pounds are set as a price upon his head.

'And further, we are too well aware that the white sails of England are presently scouring over Loch Skipport, Loch Boisdale, and the other firths around us, so that, in my humble view, a sparrow cannot escape without their knowledge and consent.

'But think not, dear Lady, for a moment that I consider my own personal danger. Certainly not, for I am ready and willing at any hour to peril my life, and to sacrifice everything personal to myself to forward the enterprise, if you think that there is even a shadow of success.'

All present felt greatly relieved by this announcement from the lips of their young and gallant friend, who seemed to be heedless of personal danger, and to be inspired with a spirit resembling that of Esther of old when she added; 'I will do all I can and if I perish, I perish.'

At Ormiclade another large meeting of friends was held at night, to plan his escape. Lady Clanranald stated that Flora had agreed to become the heroine of the dangerous enterprise.

Clanranald and his Lady, Captain O'Neil, Baileshear, and others at Ormiclade, began to put their plans into operation.

Milton, Flora's brother, although one of the friends of the Prince, was not at Ormiclade on this important occasion. He had at first intended to be there, but now pleaded indisposition as an excuse for his absence. It was, however, well known that he was a prudent, cautious man, and had no wish to be involved in perilous schemes.

On the next evening, after the meeting at Ormiclade, Flora decided to go to Milton and tell her brother of all that had been done, and the dangerous and difficult part which was allotted to herself in the enterprise. She was well aware that she would meet with his stern opposition.

Indeed she said to Lady Clanranald that, in a sense, she had a greater dread of meeting the expected disapproval of her dear and only brother than she had to face the many perils to which the whole enterpeise was exposed.

On her arrival at Milton she met her brother near the house, and at once saw the great displeasure that evidently rankled in his heart.

He addressed her sternly saying, 'What is this you are about to do, my foolish sister? Are you recklessly to submit to be made a tool of in a scheme that is, as sure as death, to terminate in ruin to yourself, to our kindred, country, and clan? Can you not see that failure in the enterprise, which will be the more probable result by far, may subject all who take part in it to the punishment of imprisonment and death?

'Just consider what Cumberland has already done by fire, and sword, and death, on the mainland; and can you, silly woman, expect to receive more mercy at his cruel hands, if found out as one of the prominent protectors of his great but unfortunate rival, Prince Charles Edward Stuart?'

Flora listened patiently to this painful address, marked all her brother's expressions with earnest attention, but remained unmoved.

After a few moments of calm reflection, and when she had observed that his feelings had somewhat subsided, she told him, 'My dear Angus, do you not believe that there is an over-ruling Providence, and a benevolent Being who has the control of all events? Take matters easy, my dear brother, and do not concern yourself about me. It will be all right, for God will prosper the adventure.'

Flora spent the night at Milton, and remained until the evening of the following day, when she set off along with her servant, Niel MacEachainn, for Ormiclade.

As she had not been furnished with a passport from any of the militia officers, she travelled at night, expecting to reach her destination in safety. In this, however, she was sadly disappointed, for in passing one of the fords on her way to Clanranald's mansion, she and her attendant, the faithful MacEachainn, were pounced upon by a party of Major Allan Macdonald's company, and detained prisoners for the night.

Major Allan was one of the most inveterate and cruel officers in the whole service against the supporters of the Prince. Flora felt very uncomfortable, dreading that she might be detained as a prisoner, and her mission aborted.

She asked one of those in the guardhouse who the officer in command was, and when he would appear there? She was informed that Captain Hugh Macdonald was in command and that he was expected to be there in the morning at an early hour.

On the arrival of the Captain, he was surprised to find his step-daughter in the guard-house. A long conversation took place between them in private, in which, no doubt, they fully discussed all the schemes and plans that were to be resorted to to secure the preservation of the Prince.

The Captain cherished the most friendly feelings towards his Royal Highness, and it was undoubtedly the desire of his heart that he might escape. Had the Captain been half as vigilant and inveterate as his Skye countryman and neighbour, Major Allan Macdonald of Knock, Charles would long before then have fallen into the relentless hands of his enemies.

The amazing secret of Betty Burke

Flora, in the hearing of the military present, subsequently addressed her step-father and informed him that she had a strong desire to go to Skye and visit her mother at Armadale, to avoid all these unpleasant encounters with the soldiers, who then ransacked every dwelling, and creek, and corner of the Long Island.

To this natural request the Captain readily agreed, and promised to get to her by that evening the necessary passports for herself, her man-servant (Niel MacEachainn), an Irish spinning-maid, named Betty Burke, and for six of a crew. Needless to say Betty Burke, the smart Irish girl, was of course Prince Charles Stuart.

Late at night the passports were handed to Flora at Ormiclade by a sergeant of Captain Macdonald's company. In addition to the passports the good Captain addressed a letter to his wife (Flora's mother) written on an unsealed sheet of paper and framed in the following terms:—

'MY DEAR MARION, — I have sent your daughter from this country, lest she should be any way frightened with the troops lying here. She has got one Betty Burke, an Irish girl, who, as she tells me, is a good spinster. If her spinning please you, you can keep her till she spin all your lint; or, if you have any wool to spin, you may employ her. I have sent Niel MacEachainn along with your daughter and Betty Burke, to take care of them. — I am, your dutiful husband,

June 22nd 1746.   HUGH MACDONALD.

Finding that the gallant heroine was now fortified with passports and plans, a number of friends met privately at Ormiclade, and with the Laird and his Lady lost no time in making every necessary and suitable arrangement. It was an evening of the deepest anxiety to all present, as the fate of the Prince depended solely on the scheme of that night.

The Prince knew little of the plans. As the hut in which Charles had been concealed was within a short distance of a military station, he deemed it prudent to shift his quarters to Rossinish, but in the process he and O'Neil nearly lost their lives. They were ignorant about the nature of the journey, and owing to the darkness of the night, they had almost fallen over a precipice.

O'Neil lost no time in acquainting his friends at Ormiclade of the Prince's new place of concealment; and in return he was instructed to acquaint his Royal Highness that all preparations were now matured, and would speedily be put into execution.

An excellent six-oared boat, the best that could be had, and six stalwart and experienced seamen, were already selected and secured, and sworn-in to be faithful. These were in readiness to meet the party at a fixed time and place.

A great portion of the evening was spent in procuring from Lady Clanranald's wardrobe suitable clothes for the poor, ragged Irish girl. The difficulty experienced was not from any scarcity of every variety of garment in the good Lady's possession, but from the uncommonly awkward, masculine-like stature of that half-famished maiden!

Whether or not she had been fed, like many of her benighted countrymen, on 'potatoes and point', is open to doubt, but whatever had been her nourishment, she exhibited such an enormous size for a young peasant female that article after article, as produced by the good Lady of Ormiclade, was cast aside by the unanimous verdict of the company as ridiculously small.

However the dress finally decided upon was one almost made up that same evening by all who could handle a needle in the house. It consisted of a flowered linen gown, sprigged with blue, a light-coloured quilted petticoat, a large cap and broad apron, and a mantle of grey-coloured camlet with a large hood, such as Irish girls were in the habit of wearing.

Next day being the 26th of June, when everything was carefully prepared, Lady Clanranald, Flora, and Niel MacEachainn, the latter of whom carried Betty Burke's dress in a well-packed bundle, were cautiously conducted by O'Neil to the miserable abode where the Prince was concealed, seven or eight miles distant from the mansion-house of Ormiclade. They arrived in safety, and found his Royal Highness alone in his wretched cave.

Supper in a cave — Flora's first meeting with the Prince

The elegant youth, the descendant of a line of kings stretching back to the remotest antiquity, was roasting kidneys and the heart and liver of a sheep for his humble repast. The sight, which was most affecting, moved the party to tears; but the natural, cheerful, and affable demeanour of the Prince soon restored his visitors to calm composure of mind.

At his request, they all sat down to partake of his cookery. The table was a flat stone resting on a pillar of turf, while the seats on which they sat were bundles of heather closely packed and tied together.

Though the fare consisted of no great variety it was substantially supplemented by a large supply of prepared meat and roasted fowls, as well as by an abundance of wine, brandy, and other acceptable eatables and viands that had just arrived from Ormiclade, as requisites for the intended voyage.

While thus seated at his table, the Prince greatly amused his guests by racy anecdotes and facetious remarks. Indeed he made himself so agreeable that all present were charmed with his affability and pleasant manners.

This was the first time Flora had ever seen him. Although the Prince had been for such a long time a hunted fugitive on that island, Flora studiously avoided meeting him until that evening.

Clanranald and his Lady had seen him frequently, and did all in their power to contribute to his comforts, but Flora had never had a sight of him, until Lady Clanranald had introduced her to him that night, as the young lady who was ready to sacrifice her life for his safety.

When the meal was over, Lady Clanranald suggested that it was now time to begin the business for which they had met, and to get the Prince disguised. To the no small amusement of all present, Flora unloosed the parcel, and produced the newly-made-up antique dress of Betty Burke. She explained to the Prince that he must now assume the character of that Irish spinning-maid, to suit the passport which she had procured for him. He laughed heartily at the idea, but thanked Flora for her ingenuity and transformed himself into Betty Burke!

A few moments later a messenger arrived, announcing that Captain Ferguson and Major Allan Macdonald, with troops of soldiers, had reached Ormiclade. It was absolutely necessary therefore that Lady Clanranald should hasten home to avoid suspicion. She accordingly took an affectionate leave of the Prince, and left the heroic Flora, Captain O'Neil, and Niel MacEachainn to pass the night with him.

It was now a period of indescribable anxiety, yet the soul of Flora felt no fear. She rose superior to the dire emergency of that eventful evening, and in none of the trying scenes of her chequered life does she appear to more advantage than in her firmness and mental determination in the presence of the Prince and his friends, after the departure of Lady Clanranald.

Captain O'Neil, who had been the inseparable companion of his Royal Highness, insisted on accompanying him from the island, while the Prince, in turn, refused to be separated from his faithful friend. At this juncture Flora addressed the Prince and told him in a firm, determined tone, that such a proposal was utterly and clearly impracticable! She spoke respectfully, but very decidedly.

'Your Royal Highness must at once understand', she said, 'that as I procured passports for three persons only; that is, one each for myself and my servant, and one for my mother's spinning-maid, the attempt of a fourth to escape without a passport, and especially so Captain O'Neil, a gentleman so well known to every officer and soldier all over the island, would jeopardise the lives of us all.'

To this firm reasoning the Prince and O'Neil yielded at once, although, no doubt, with considerable reluctance. About midnight Flora, Captain O'Neil, and Niel MacEachainn took leave of the Prince and left him to meditate in his lonely solitude.

Flora made the best of her way to bid farewell to her brother, as the coming evening was the one appointed for the attempt to get across to Skye.

Captain O'Neil was that morning arrested by a party of the military on his way to Ormiclade, and made prisoner.

When Lady Clanranald had arrived at her own home she was questioned by General Campbell and Captain Ferguson, who demanded to know where she had been, when she left home, and what was the cause of her absence? She replied with firm composure, that she had a very good reason for her absence, and one that caused her much grief; that she was visiting a dear dying friend.

And it was true that she did call on her way home upon a young lady suffering in the last stages oif a fatal disease.

About ten o'clock at night on the following evening, being Friday, June 27, 1746, the Prince, Flora and Niel MacEachainn proceeded to the sea-shore, to the place where it was previously arranged they should meet the boat. On their arrival, wet and weary, as the rain fell in torrents, they observed to their horror several small vessels or wherries, filled with armed men, sailing within a gunshot of the spot where they lay concealed.

Fortunately, however, these objects of terror tacked in an opposite direction, and soon disappeared in the hazy gloom.

Their perilous voyage across the Minch to Skye

About an hour later their own boat rowed up gently with muffled oars to the spot where they were so anxiously awaiting it. With all possible speed they embarked on their perilous voyage across the Minch to Skye, a distance of between thirty-five and forty miles.

The Prince was more anxious to get to Skye than any quarter on the mainland, as that Island was almost entirely the property of two clans, the Macdonalds and Macleods, both of whom were ostensibly hostile to the Jacobite cause. On this account Cumberland had sent few of his Government troops to occupy it, and watch the movements of strangers.

Charles was likewise well aware that he had a warm and faithful friend in Lady Margaret, the wife of Sir Alexander Macdonald of Sleat, whose kindness his Royal Highness had already experienced.

The voyage was perilous in the extreme, as the whole channel was scoured by Government vessels, eager to arrest the Prince dead or alive. It was with them, however, now 'to do or die', and the attempt had to be made.

At first the breeze was moderate and favourable, but in a few hours one of those sudden summer storms, so common in these Isles unexpectedly blew up. The wind roared in terrific gusts, the billows rolled mountains high, threatening to engulf their small craft.

To make matters worse, one of those thunderstorms with which the Hebrideans are so familiar set in, and at one time the party became painfully alarmed as to their safety.

Their boat was an open one, about twenty-four feet keel, but one of the best that the Long Island could furnish. The crew were sturdy, well-picked men, and excellent seamen, well skilled in managing their craft in a storm, and yet that night they had much to do.

Their utmost energies were called forth to manage their boat amid the raging billows. They had no compass, and when less than two hours at sea, the storm increased to such a terrific degree, that the ocean was lashed into deep, foaming waves.

At that moment, as if to add to their already indescribable

terror, thunder rolled in rattling peals over their heads, while the lightning flashed from cloud to cloud in the murky atmosphere. The crew had to steer before the wind, which frequently shifted, and for hours they were entirely at the mercy of the raging elements.

Yet they did their work calmly and steadily, though at times they instinctively exclaimed to one another — 'Ochan! is Ochan! is e tha garbh! is e tha garbh.' 'Alas! Alas; it is rough; it is rough' — and so it was.

The Prince all along behaved nobly. He cheered the seamen by relating anecdotes and by singing verses of sea-songs. Poor Flora, anxious and tired, and no doubt alive to the many dangers that surrounded her, became overpowered with sleep. She lay on the ballast of the boat wrapped in a plaid, and the Prince kept watch to prevent her slumbers from being disturbed.

At break of day they were greatly perplexed at seeing no land in any direction — nothing visible but the azure horizon all round, and without a compass they did not know how to direct their craft. The storm had by this time fortunately moderated, and while the seamen had been steering at random for so many hours, their hearts were at last cheered, when in the dim distance the lofty headlands of Skye came into view.

They made speedily for the shore, and soon approached the Point of Waternish, a promontory on the north-west coast of that island. But they were dismayed, on drawing near the land, to see a large party of the Macleod Militia on the beach waiting their arrival!

The crew immediately cried with one simultaneous shout — 'Mach i! Mach i! Mach i! air ball!' — 'Out with her! Out with her! to sea with her immediately!' — and with a few desperate pulls the boat was soon rowed beyond the reach of the red-coats on the shore.

The militia, sadly disappointed, and having no boat fit to pursue, fired a shower of bullets after them, which fortunately did no injury, though the balls struck and riddled their sails. The danger was indeed great, for one of the balls cleft the handle of

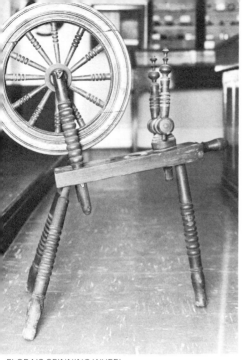

FLORA'S SPINNING WHEEL

FLORA from a portrait painted by
W. Robertson in Life in 1750

THE PRINCE'S ARMY PASSING LOCH EIL (1745)

CHARLES AS BETTY BURKE

the helm, and grazed one of the steerman's fingers, but did no further injury. |

The Prince stood up and cheered the crew, and told them not to mind the fellows ashore, but to continue bravely doing their duty.

Bullets whizz past their ears . . . .

During the rapid firing of the militia, he was endeavouring to persuade Flora to recline in the bottom of the boat; but she refused, unless the Prince, whose life she considered far more valuable than her own, would take the same precaution.

Eventually as the danger increased, and as the bullets whizzed past close to their ears, the Prince, Flora and Neil squatted down all three on the ballast flags, and continued in that position until the boat was beyond the reach of danger.

Early on the afternoon of Saturday they landed safely at a place called Kilbride, in the parish of Kilmuir, and within five hundred yards of the house of Monkstadt, the residence of Sir Alexander Macdonald of the Isles.

There was at this time a small cave under a shelving rock at Kilbride, which was beyond the high-water mark, and the Prince took shelter in it, making a seat of Flora's trunk, which was carried from the boat for that purpose. This cave has since been demolished by the removal of stones from it for building purposes.

After the Prince, Flora, and the faithful Niel, had been safely landed, the crew rowed the boat into an adjoining creek, where they expected to have enjoyed some rest and food. Flora, accompanied by her servant Niel, walked at once to Monkstadt House, while for a short time the Prince was alone in his solitary cave.

> 'Tis midnight: a lone boat is on the sea,
> And dark clouds gather, but no thoughts of fear
> Chill those brave hearts! A princely refugee
> Disguised — a faithful maiden sitting near,
> Upon whose cheek anon there falls a tear —

Fond woman's pledge of sympathy. A crew,
Trusty and gallant, labour at the oars.
The shifting wind white showers of spray uprears
Like incense heavenward; the water roars,
While from huge murky clouds the lurid lightning pours!

Sir Alexander Macdonald, who refused to support the cause of the Prince, was fortunately away from home at this time, otherwise his presence might have been a restraint on the benevolence of his Lady, a staunch Jacobite at heart. The worthy Baronet was then at Fort Augustus in attendance upon the Duke of Cumberland.

It was fortunate, however, that Lady Margaret was at home. She was a lady noted for her great beauty and accomplishments.

On the arrival of Flora and her attendant at Monkstadt, she requested one of the servants to tell Lady Margaret that she had just called on her way from the Long Island. The heroine was at once shown into the drawing-room, where she found several gentlemen sitting, in military dress, among whom was Captain John Macleod, son of Donald Macleod of Balmeanach, who was in command of a band of militia, then stationed at Uig, about two miles distant. Others of Macleod's men were also in the house at the time.

A lady friend of Flora was also present, Mrs Macdonald, the wife of John Macdonald of Kirkibost, North Uist, who arrived a few days before from the Long Island, and who had informed Lady Margaret privately, that, in all probability, the Prince would soon land in Skye.

Among the rest Flora was delighted to meet her good old friend, Mr Alexander Macdonald of Kingsburgh, *alias* 'Alasdair Macdhomhnuill Mhic Alasdair Mhic Ailein', factor for Sir Alexander.

When Flora entered the rather crowded room, the whole company arose to welcome her, as, owing to her long absence in Edinburgh, they had not seen her for years. She was amiable and cheerful, and warmly exchanged the congratulations of her respected friends.

Her acute perception, however, led her to suspect that Captain Macleod had an idea in his mind, that her appearance on this occasion was caused by something more important than a mere friendly visit. Under this impression she entered into a free and easy conversation with him, sat beside him, and appeared delighted with his social talk.

His conduct towards her was for a time of a very different kind, and indeed scarcely courteous. His language bordered on rudeness, and the questions put by him were positively uncivil.

Flora keeps a secret

'Be pleased to tell me, my good lady, whence you came today, whither do you intend to go — by what boat or vessel did you cross the Minch, and who accompanied you?'

To all these pointed queries the gallant maiden, smiling and self-possessed, returned distinct replies in calm and pleasing language; and her deportment was so fascinating and agreeable throughout, that she soon won upon the impertinent officer, at once gained his esteem, and had the honour of being escorted by him to dinner, where she received his most assiduous attention.

The questions now asked her were of a less disagreeable character, such as — 'What news, Miss Macdonald, from the Long Island? What of that unfortunate rebel, Prince Charles?'

In answer to the latter, Flora smiled and expressed herself in the blandest terms, saying, 'Perhaps, Captain Macleod, you are not aware that I am a bit of a Jacobite myself, and I am therefore glad to understand, that the unfortunate fugitive has at last succeeded in effecting his escape from his pursuers, and that, by means of a vessel from France put at his service, he has left the Long Island.'

The officer listened attentively, and deemed the truth of the statement highly probable.

At dinner, Lady Margaret sat at the head of the table, and her factor, Kingsburgh, in the absence of her husband, occupied the other end of it. As the guests were numerous, and some of them, such as Flora and Mrs Macdonald, Kirkibost, exceptionally welcome ones, her Ladyship appeared overjoyed. But she was not aware that the Prince was in the immediatte vicinity of her dwelling.

Shortly after dinner Flora managed to get hold of Kingsburgh alone, and told him all about the Prince, and suggested the necessity of his breaking the news to Lady Margaret, as she could not venture to do it herself, in case she might become so affected by her Ladyship's probable alarm. Kingsburgh being a cool and sensible gentleman, undertook to perform this important but delicate duty.

Half-an-hour later he took her Ladyship into a private apartment, and revealed the secret to her. Her reaction was to fall into a fit of hysterics.

She expressed herself in accents of terror — sat trembling on a chair, and exclaimed — 'Oh! dear Kingsburgh, we are undone — we are ruined — we will all have to suffer the penalty of death on the scaffold! O dear! O dear! what is this?'

Kingsburgh, with characteristic prudence and serenity of mind, assured her that there was no danger whatever, that he himself would conduct his Royal Highness to Kingsburgh House, and that all would be right in the end.

'Oh', said her Ladyship, 'how much I wish that my dear, sterling friend, Captain Donald Roy were here at this moment. I sent him the other day to Fladda-chuain (an island in the Minch), as I was told the Prince was expected to land there, and he was supplieed with shirts and other requisites for his comfort.

'I hope that he has returned to Shulista, where he is a patient of Dr Maclean, for the curing of his leg, pierced by a musket ball in the battle of Culloden. He may now be at home, let him get notice to come immediately.'

Donald Roy was accordingly sent for, and soon arrived on horseback at Monkstadt. He found Lady Margaret and Kingsburgh walking alone in the garden. By this time they had less reserve, as Captain Macleod and his men had gone to Uig to visit their company of military stationed there.

Lady Margaret was greatly cheered by the presence of Donald Roy, though she could not help saying to him — 'I fear, my dear Donald, that it is all over with us, and that we are ruined for ever.'

'There is not the least fear of that, my Lady, take comfort, as all will succeed well', replied Donald.

By this time Flora made her appearance, with an air of smiling cheerfulness; and her conversation and presence restored her Ladyship to a calm and collected state of mind. They now held a consultation to adopt plans for the morning.

They agreed to send Niel MacEachainn to tell Charles that Kingsburgh proposed to visit him on the shore very soon. Niel at once performed this duty and speedily returned.

Kingsburgh soon arrived at the cave with some brandy and wine for the Prince, as well as something substantial to eat, but there was no sign of the Prince. Niel who was in advance, awaited Kingsburgh's arrival, and remained in charge of the refreshments, while Kingsburgh set off in search of Charles, and walked across the fields in the direction of the house of Scuddeburgh.

En route he saw in the distance a giant-like figure in female attire, stalking rapidly over the meadow. Kingsburgh caught up with the female and established 'her' true identity.

Late in the evening Sir Alexander's cattleman entered the servants' hall at Monkstadt, in a very excited state, and declared:— 'Lord, preserve us! I saw a large female quickly traversing the fields betwixt this and the fort, with a long stick in her hand, with a curious hood on her head, and with a remarkable dress on her person. Undoubtedly she must be one of those whom the Fairies had locked up in their chambers in the fort, who contrived to escape. I never beheld one to be compared with her in the shape of a worldly creature.'

Kingsburgh related this anecdote to the Prince, who heartily laughed at it.

Niel MacEachainn informed the astonished cattleman, as well as the other menials present, that the gigantic female in question was no fairy prisoner in Scuddeburgh Fort, but an Irish spinning-maid whom they had ferried from the Long Island, on her way to the home of Flora Macdonald's mother, at Armadale.

The Prince was now left for the night in a recess
on the shore to which Niel had carried blankets and other coverings to afford him comfort.

Meanwhile Captain Macleod and his companions returned from Uig to Monkstadt, and had retired for the night. This circumstance afforded the Prince's friends a better opportunity for getting on with their schemes.

The midnight plot

Lady Margaret, Flora, and old Kingsburgh, with Captain Donald Roy Macdonald, assembled after midnight in a private room. It was arranged that Kingsburgh should take the Prince next morning to his own house, twelve miles distant, and then pass him on through Skye to the Island of Raasay. It was further arranged that Donald Roy should that very night make the 20 mile trip to Portree, the capital of Skye, and send for the young laird of Raasay, who would provide a boat to ferry the Prince to that Island.

When all was ready, and after shaking hands with Lady Margaret, Captain Macleod and others, Flora and Mrs Macdonald trotted away. The faithful Niel MacEachainn, and two other young men who were well acquainted with the hill riding-path, accompanied them on foot. Moving slowly along, the party, after a few hours, overtook Kingsburgh and his Irish maid.

By then, however, the unceasing rain fell in such torrents as to swell the mountain streams to overflowing, and render most of the usual fords almost impassable. Here and there under the shelter of rocks, the party rested to pass the time. Having arrived at a pretty spot, they were directed to a pure spring of water, at which they sat down, and mingled part of its contents with Lady Margaret's mountain-dew.

The well had been pointed out to the drenched party by the boy who was herding cattle at the place, and who, for his assistance, received from the big Irish woman his first ever shilling. His name was John Macdonald, a smart raw-boned lad, bonnetless, and barefooted, who could not talk a word of English.

He lived to the great age of one hundred and seven years, and died in Lawnmarket, Edinburgh, in 1835, at the house of his son, Donald Macdonald, bagpipe maker to the Highland Society of Scotland.

Several ludicrous incidents took place on this rough and uncomfortable journey. Again and again Betty Burke, forgetting her assumed sex, when leaping over streams, and climbing rugged cliffs, managed her ragged skirts with amusing awkwardness.

Chambers in his description of this journey informs us that:— 'In crossing a stream which traversed the road, Charles held up his petticoats indelicately high, to save them from being wet. Kingsburgh pointed out that, by doing so he must excite strange suspicions among those who should happen to see him; and his Royal Highness promised to take better care on the next occasion. Accordingly in crossing another stream, he permitted his skirts to hang down and float upon the water.

'Kingbsurgh again represented that this mode was as likely as the other to attract attention; and the Prince could not help laughing at the difficulty of adjusting this trifling and yet important matter of his dress.'

In the afternoon the party were met by numbers of country people returning home from church, who stared at the uncommon size and slovenly appearance of that Irish lass that strode so reckless-like along! Kingsburgh upbraided them for their unmannerly curiosity, yet, they exclaimed in astonishment: — 'Oh! see that strange woman! Behold the big, wide steps of that rude, long-legged dame! Eh me! what a bold, untidy, slovenly, uncouth slattern she is! Surely she must be one of the giant race!'

The poor peasants were utterly bewildered, as well they might be!

After an uncomfortable day's travelling, the party arrived in safety at the mansion of Kingsburgh, a little before midnight. They had no desire to reach it earlier.

The family had all gone to rest. Kingsburgh sent Flora and a servant maid to his wife's bedroom to get her up so she could prepare a supper for her husband and his guests.

While the meal was being prepared by Mrs Macdonald, Flora stood beside her, and related her adventures of the previous two days. The lady remarked that Flora had acted very imprudently in allowing the boat that brought them to Skye to return immediately to the Long Island, as on its arrival, the crew could not escape being seized, and questioned closely. The consequence would no doubt be, that the Royal troops would set out in fresh pursuit.

She was proved right, for the boat on its return was instantly captured. Captain Ferguson immediately set sail in his Government cutter for Skye, and pursued the track of the Prince from his landing at Monkstadt, until he finally escaped from the Island. This merciless officer was, however, a week too late.

The oversight of allowing the boat to return so soon to Uist, was the only point in which the judgment of Flora had ever failed. It is true that she did not suggest or sanction its return, but, unfortunately, she did not give instruction to the contrary; and the crew were no doubt eager to return to their homes.

Meantime, Mrs Macdonald of Kingsburgh, assisted by Flora, and Mrs Macdonald, Kirkibost, prepared supper, at which the Prince sat on the right of the hostess, and Flora on her left. After supper, to which the Prince did ample justice, the ladies retired, leaving Kingsburgh and his august guest alone.

His Royal Highness, apologising for the liberty, produced a small, black, tobacco pipe, which he called 'the cutty', and was enjoying a puff from it, while his host prepared hot water, sugar, and mountain dew to make a bowl of toddy. He was extremely cheerful, and while enjoying the exhilarating contents of the magic bowl, he assured Kingsburgh that he had never tasted such excellent toddy in his life. He thought that it excelled by far what he had at Borrodale and in the Long Island.

He indeed greatly enjoyed himself, after his many fatigues

and hardships, and had no desire as yet to retire to bed. Kingsburgh, however, seeing the wisdom and necessity of Charles getting rest, had to perform the disagreeable duty of suggesting the propriety of breaking up the company, but the prince objected.

'After thay had emptied the bowl several times,' as Chambers graphically describes, 'Kingsburgh thought it necessary to hint to the Prince that, as he would require to be up and away as soon as possible on the morrow, he had better now go to bed, so that he might enjoy a proper term of sleep. To his surprise, Charles was by no means anxious for rest.

'On the contrary, he insisted upon another bowl, that they might, as he said, finish their conversation. Kingsburgh refused but Charles demanded more drink. After some good-humoured altercation, when Kingsburgh took away the bowl to put it by, his Royal Highness rose to detain it, and a struggle ensued, in which the little vessel broke in two pieces, Charles retaining one in his hands, and Kingsburgh holding the other.

'The strife was thus brought to an end, and the Prince no longer objected to go to bed.'

He slept soundly until two in the afternoon, when Kingsburgh entered his bedroom, and told him that it was time to get up, have breakfast, and prepare for the journey to Portree, a distance of about eight miles.

About three in the afternoon the Prince set off on his journey, accompanied by Flora, and the dutiful Niel MacEachainn. Niel carried with him the substantial Highland dress of a farmer, and a pair of new shoes, all of which Kingsburgh had provided for his Royal Highness. These were to be exchanged for the Irish dress at some convenient distance from the house.

About half-a-mile on their way, Flora walked on, while the Prince and Niel entered a hollow between two rocks, where Charles robed himself in his new dress and shoes. Niel, at the same time, carefully preserved and concealed the tattered raiment, and torn 'bachules' of Betty Burke, as keepsakes for Kingsburgh of the Prince's perilous adventures.

Captain Donald Roy reached Portree on the previous evening and having met young Raasay at the farmhouse of Toutrome, they prepared everything for meeting the distinguished pair from Kingsburgh, and for conveying the Prince to the Island of Raasay.

Sadness as Prince bids Flora last farewell

When the Prince and his attendants arrived, they went to the only inn in the village with young Raasay and Donald Roy to procure refreshments. Donald suggested the propriety of the Prince's retiring to a place of safety, as there was great danger in remaining longer in a public hostelry, when so many spies and suspicious charaters were moving about.

He told him that he knew of a cave where he could find shelter until removed under cover of night to Raasay. They all left the inn immediately, except Flora, under a drenching rain.

The time had now come when Charles had to part forever with his true and faithful protectress, the gallant Flora. With tears in his eyes he laid hold of the heroine's hands, and bade her a tender and affecting farewell.

He thanked her for enabling him to escape and handed her his portrait in a golden locket. Then he tenderly saluted her, and said, in affecting tones, that he yet hoped to meet her at the Court of St James, where he should be able properly to reward her self-denying heroism — and her ardent devotion and loyalty to her unfortunate Prince.

Such were the adventures of only three days, which have immortalised the name of Flora and for ever shed a halo of glory over the devotedness of the female heart. But although the Prince lived for upwards of forty-two years after this parting scene on the beach of Portree, he never acknowledged by letter or otherwise the dangers to which Flora exposed herself to save his life. It was a snub which baffled his many admirers.

During the darkness of that night he was conveyed from his cave to Raasay, and then through Skye to the mainland, where for nearly three months he had to undergo terrible trials and severe hardships. His home was in rocks and caves, and in mountain recesses, where he passed his weary time hourly exposed and liable to be seized by his vigilant pursuers.

At last, fortunately for him, two French vessels, the 'L'Heureux' and the 'Princesse de Conti', arrived at Loch nan Uagh. He got aboard and sailed for France on September 20, 1746.

He died, after having spent a chequered, but by no means a too provident career, on January 30, 1788.

Flora is taken prisoner

When the authorities learned of Flora's role in the affair she was taken to London, where she was kept as a State prisoner for nearly twelve months.

An Act of Indemnity was eventually passed, when she was freed and permitted to return to her native Highland hills. Greater attention could not be paid to any lady, than was paid to her by all classes of the nobility, in London and elsewhere; yet her gentle heart longed for the homely welcome which she knew awaited her from her friends in Skye, and in the Long Island.

Before Flora was taken from Skye to London, she encountered many difficulties. In a short time the various movements of the Prince through Skye, Raasay, and other adjacent localities became known; and the finger was soon pointed at those who had helped him get away.

Flora was considered the chief actor in this hazardous adventure. She had, however, a great number of faithful accomplices. Among them were Clanranald and his lady; Donald Roy Macdonald, brother of Hugh Macdonald of Baileshear; Donald Macleod of Galtrigal, Malcolm Macleod, Old Kingsburgh, and several others.

Of all these, none could be more sincere and true to the Prince in his misfortunes than Donald Macleod of Galtrigal. He was a shrewd, ingenious man.

When details of his role in helping Charles escape reached offical ears Donald was arrested in Benbecula and taken to

London. He was released in June of the following year, when Mr John Walkinshaw presented him with a handsome silver snuff-box, beautifully chased and gilt.

Donald was one of those well-to-do farmers in Skye, who at that period lived comfortably on their comparatively small tenements and paid then from £30 to £60 of rent.

As soon as it became known for certain that Prince Charles had succeeded in making his way to France, the Royal forces scattered over the Western Isles became greatly annoyed. They were determined to wreak their vengeance on the various actors who had assisted the Prince to elude their grasp.

Kingsburgh's involvement was discovered by the Captain of one of the Government ships. That venerable old gentleman was consequently arrested, sent a prisoner to Fort Augustus, and then to Edinburgh Castle, where he was treated with painful severity and cruelty for a whole year.

It was a maid employed by Kingsburgh who unwittingly spilled the beans about him giving Charles shelter to Captain Ferguson of the Government warship, investigating a rumour that the Prince had escaped to Skye.

Lulled into conversation by the smooth talking Captain, and dazzled by gifts and a tour of his ship, the girl disclosed, with an air of unpardonable pride, that she had seen Prince Charles, that he'd spent a night at her master's house, and that his appearance pleased her very much. She added that the Prince's shoes were all torn, that he wore a *cota-clo* (that is a kelt coat) that belonged to Mr Allan, her master's son.

This was all that Ferguson wanted, and in consequence of the girl's imprudent disclosure, the Government officials obtained the first direct proof of the Prince's motions, and of the manner in which Kingsburgh had acted in securing his escape.

On the same day on which the Prince left Kingsburgh House for Portree, the old gentleman, sensing danger, crossed the hill to the east side of the island, but his pursuers soon discovered him at a place called *Lealt.* Young Allan, however, managed all along to elude the Government officers and was never captured.

Flora, on the other hand, with her natural gallantry, made no attempts whatever to conceal herself. After having parted with the Royal fugitive at Portree, she went to spend a few days with her mother at Armadale, and then made the rest of her way to her brother's residence at Milton.

She had been there only a few days when she received a summons to appear for examination before Macleod of Talisker, a Captain of Militia, in the Isle of Skye, to answer 'grave charges'

Her friends became alarmed and told her to ignore the summons. They wanted her to go into hiding but she refused, saying with her natural magnaminity of soul that as she had done nothing of which she either repented or felt ashamed, she would appear at any tribunal or before any Government official, and answer whatever charges might be brought against her.

Unprotected and alone she set out for Talisker, and Captain Macleod, when satisfied by the various statements which he had elicited from the gentle culprit before him, permitted her to visit her mother at Armadale.

On her way, she accidentally met with her stepfather returning from the Long Island, and before evening she was seized by a party of soldiers, who took her prisoner on board the *Furnace,* commanded by Captain Ferguson.

General Campbell, who happened to be on board, treated the amiable rebel with great kindness and consideration. He allowed her to land at Armadale, under an escort of soldiers, to bid farewell to her mother, to replenish her wardrobe, and to procure a female servant, Kate Macdonald.

Meantime her stepfather, the officer of militia who granted passports to Flora, Betty Burke, and the others, to cross from the Long Island to Skye, became afraid that he might be implicated in the plot, and fled into hiding. Had not this officer granted the requisite passports, the gallant Flora could never have conducted the Prince from Uist to Skye. These passports were the documents on which the success of the whole adventure depended.

Flora, now a State prisoner of great importance, was conveyed from Skye on board the *Furnace* to Dunstaffnage Castle, in Argyll, where she was confined for about ten days, under the charge of Mr Neil Campbell, at the time the Governor of that ancient Castle. It was once a royal residence of the Kings of Scotland, and is situated on a rocky promontory that juts out into Loch Etive.

General Campbell sent the following note to the Governor, introducing his 'very pretty young rebel':—

Horse Shoe Bay, 1st August, 1746

Dear Sir — I must desire the favour of you to forward my letters by an express to Inveraray; and if any are left with you, let them be sent by the bearer. I shall stay here with Commodore Smith till Sunday morning. If you can't come, I beg to know if you have any men now in garrison at your house, and how many? Make my compliments to your lady, and tell her that I am obliged to desire the favour of her for some days to receive a very pretty young rebel. Her zeal, and the persuasion of those who ought to have given her better advice, have drawn her into a most unhappy scrape, by assisting the young Pretender to make his escape. I need say nothing further till we meet; only assure you that I am, dear Sir, your sincere friend, and humble servant,

JOHN CAMPBELL

P.S. — I suppose you have heard of Miss Flora Macdonald? —J.C.

To Neil Campbell, Esq, Captain of Dunstaffnage.

About ten days after, General Campbell addressed another brief note to the same Governor, in the following terms:—

Wednesday Evening

Sir, — You will deliver to the bearer, John Macleod, Miss Macdonald, to be conducted in his wherry. Having no officer to send, it would be very proper you send one of your garrison alongst with her. — I am, Sir, your most obedient humble servant,

JOHN CAMPBELL

To the Captain of Dunstaffnage.

During our heroine's short stay at this fortress, the Governor's lady, and other friends, paid her every possible attention. All of them were struck by Flora's accomplished manners and humble deportment. Her society was courted and appreciated by all the respectable families in the neighbourhood, who had been privately invited to meet her as a distinguished State prisoner.

When John Macleod and his wherry arrived to take her away, it was late in the evening; but next morning the preparations for departure were made. After an early breakfast, the Governor's lady, with tears in her eyes, handed Flora into the boat.

The sails were immediately set, and before a stiff breeze, the frail craft glided swiftly down Loch Etive, towards the Sound of Mull, and soon disappeared.

It is probable that John Macleod and the Dunstaffnage officer conveyed Miss Flora to Glasgow, as some days afterwards our fair captive was put on board the *Bridgewater,* commanded by Commodore Smith, in Leith Roads. During the detention of the *Bridgewater,* at this port, for nearly three months, Flora's fame had spread far and near, and she became the object of much public interest.

On board Flora met Captain O'Neil, and several other of her countrymen who had, like herself, been arrested for the same cause.

The Commander and all the inferior officers vied with each other in offering civility to their interesting prisoner. Though she was not permitted to leave the vessel, persons of every rank, clerical and lay, and of all shades of politics, were freely allowed to go on board to visit her.

Day after day hundreds of the aristocracy flocked to see the spirited young lady, and many valuable gifts were made to her, as tokens of their esteem. Among those visitors, the clergymen of Edinburgh and Leith of almost every denomination paid their respects to her.

The quiet demeanour of the heroine during the vessel's stay

at Leith was admired by all who had seen her. The Episcopal clergymen of the place described her, and the scenes on board, in these terms: — 'Some', said he, 'that went on board to pay their respects to her used to take a dance in the cabin, and to press her much to share with them in the diversion, but with all their importunity, they could not prevail with her to take a trip.

'She told them at present her dancing days were done, and she would not readily entertain a thought of that diversion until she could be assured of her Prince's safety, and perhaps not till she should be blessed with the happiness of seeing him again.

'Although she was easy and cheerful, yet she had a certain mixture of gravity in all her behaviour, which became her situation exceedingly well, and set her off to great advantage. She is of a low stature, of a fair complexion, and well enough shaped.

'One would not discern by her conversation that she had spent all her former days in the Highlands, for she talks English easily, and not at all through the Erse tone. She has a sweet voice, and sings well; and no lady, Edinburgh bred, can acquit herself better at the tea-table, than what she did when in Leith Roads.

'Her wise conduct in one of the most perplexing scenes that can happen in life — her fortitude and good sense — are memorable instances of the strength of a female mind, even in those years that are tender and inexperienced.'

Flora faces a charge of treason

On November 7, 1746, the *Bridgewater* weighed anchor amid the display of flags and the cheers of thousands, to carry the fair prisoner and others to London, to stand trial on a charge of treason.

But Flora's romantic story had caught the imagination and support of Londoners and the Government realised it dared not risk widespread public opposition by confining her in an ordinary prison. So, after a short stay in the Tower, with many others from the Western Isles, who had been engaged in the same cause, she was handed over to the custody of friends who became responsible to the Government for her appearance when demanded.

In this mitigated imprisonment Flora remained a State prisoner for nearly twelve months, until, in 1747, the Act of Indemnity was passed, and she was set at liberty.

Throughout those months she maintained a cheerful temper, an easy, elegant, and winning address, and appeared most agreeable to all her visitors. Immediately after she received her freedom, she became the guest of Lady Primrose of Dunnipace, where she was visited, and loaded with honours, by distinguished persons of all ranks and classes of the nobility.

All admired the dauntless part she had acted, and her case excited so much interest, that she had the honour of a visit from Frederick, Prince of Wales. His Royal Highness asked her how she dared to assist a rebel against his father's throne when she replied, with great simplicity but firmness, that she would have done the same thing for him had she found him in similar distress.

The Prince was so struck with this reply and her manner, that he afterwards ensured she received every comfort.

Meanwhile, the street in which Lady Primrose lived was, day after day, thronged with the carriages of folk who wanted to see Flora. Artists waited upon her to paint her portrait, others to award their gifts; and altogether Flora could never understand how such sa simple act of humanity should produce so much excitement, or confer upon her, what she considered, such unmerited fame.

When her liberation was announced, and when made aware that she was freely privileged to return to her native Highlands, she respectfully solicited as a special favour, that her fellow-prisoners from the Western Isles should receive the same liberty as herself. She won freedom for old Kingsburgh, Donald

Macleod of Galtrigal, *Calum Mac Iain Mhic Iain,* who went in the capacity of guide to the Prince from the Island of Raasay to Kilmorie, in Strathaird, and also of Neil Macdonald, her servant, who subsequently followed the Prince to France.

This task accomplished, Flora, with her faithful *Nial Mac Eachainn,* left London in a coach and four for Edinburgh.

During the journey of several days, the exuberance of Niel's spirits could hardly be restrained. He was naturally an active, lively, and manly youth, possessed of considerable wit, and no small share of poetic genius. He, as well as most of his companions, never expected to return.

It is related that Old Kingsburgh, despairing of ever again seeing his family and home, made a hasty will of all his effects before he left Skye.

The gallant Flora herself was the most hopeful that no injury would befall her, and that her personal safety stood in no danger. She reasoned in this way; that she had done nothing wrong, and that all her actions in that great tragedy of her life were based, not on political principles, but on the Scriptural laws of humanity and kindness.

On the arrival of the party in Edinburgh, Flora remained with kind friends for about three weeks, retaining her faithful valet, Niel MacEachainn, and the Skye girl, Kate Macdonald, as her trusty bodyguards. During her stay she lived very much in privacy. She had been wearied with the amount of attention previously paid to her.

From Edinburgh she made the best of her way to Inverness, where she had some respected friends, who made her their quest for about ten days.

Hugh Macdonald, her stepfather at Armadale in Skye, sent a horse and saddle to convey her to her mother's house, where she arrived in safety.

She complained of nothing particularly except her fingers, which were blistered and bleeding from holding the bridle on such a rough and lenthened journey.

Having satisfied her mother with full and particular details of all her adventures and perils, she took leave of her for a time, that she might once more have the pleasure of visiting Lady Clanranald at Ormiclade, and her brother at Milton, in Uist.

Nearly two months had, however, elapsed before she accomplished this journey, because of stop-offs along the way. She visited her friends at Scalpa, Raasay, Scorriebreck, Kingsburgh, Flodigarry, and specially at Monkstadt, where Lady Margaret and Sir Alexander Macdonald rejoiced at her appearance.

On her arrival at Scorriebreck, near Portree, where she parted with the Prince, Mr Nicolson, tenant of Scorriebreck, and his lady, welcomed her with marked enthusiasm.

After a stay there of a few days, Mr Nicolson invited a large party of the neighbouring ladies to meet the distinguished stranger. Among the rest was Major Allan Macdonald *(Ailean a' Chnoic),* who had, by a cunning device, arrested Flora's friend, Donald Macleod of Galtrigal, and was the cause of his imprisonment.

Flora delivers a broadside

When the Major entered the drawing-room, and received the ordinary congratulations of the company, he held out his hand to Flora, whereupon she tartly expressed herself — 'Yes, Sir, I give you my hand, but not entirely with my heart. I wish to show all courtesy to the profession which you have disgraced by a low and base stratagem, utterly unworthy of the conduct of a soldier, a Highlander, and a gentleman!' This piquant repartee, for a moment, paralysed the whole company.

Having made a few other visits to respectable families in the neighbourhood of Portree, where all were delighted to see her, Flora went to the mansion house of Kingsburgh, the residence of her future father-in-law, Mr Alexander Macdonald, but found on her arrival that the old gentleman, who had but lately returned from his imprisonment in Edinburgh Castle, had gone to Flodigarry, in the north end of the Island. where his son, Allan, lived.

Flora, impatient to see Lady Margaret, set off on horseback, and in litle more than an hour, arrived at the residence of her chief, at Monkstadt. She was warmly embraced by her Ladyship, with whom she had always been a great favourite.

A few days after her arrival at Monkstadt she was taken suddenly and seriously ill. Lady Margaret became painfully alarmed, and despatched an express for Sir Alexander, at the time on a visit to Dunvegan Castle. Without a moment's delay, the only medical man in the Island was sent for, and the first illness under which the devoted Flora had ever been known to suffer, caused much anxiety in the whole family.

Fortunately, however, before either Sir Alexander or the medical attendant arrived, she began to rally as speedily as she had been taken ill.

During her stay at Monkstadt, which lasted more than three weeks, the house was frequented by a great many visitors and guests. Sir Alexander, in honour of his fair namesake, staged a splendid banquet, to which all the principal families in the Island were invited, together with a number of the Government officers still sojourning in Skye.

The festivities extended over four days, when high and low were entertained in a manner that did credit to the friendly generosity and hospitality of the great *Mac Dhomhnuill* of the Isles. Among the party were Flora's brother from Milton, Clanranald, and his lady.

It was on this occasion that the arrangements were made, chiefly by Lady Margaret, for Flora's marriage with Allan Macdonald, Kingsburgh's son. For some years before, when Flora and her intended were in their teens, it was well known to their friends that an attachment existed between them.

Lady Margaret, at a friendly party in the house one evening, jocularly conversed about this alliance, saying, in her well-known frank and affable manner, that about-to-be married people were always subjects for speculation, and that on this occasion she was to speculate a little herself. One thing, she said, was apparent, that Allan and Flora resembled one another in tempers, characters, and ages — and they even resembled each other in person — and that they were no doubt intended for one another.

Flora modestly replied, that the step her Ladyship alluded to was the most important in a woman's life; but she could not think of such an event taking place for two or three years to come.

The fact was that Flora's judgment was of a practical kind, and her prudence possessed a masculine strength while tempered with feminine delicacy. She knew well that the nature of old Kingsburgh's duties as a public functionary, however honourable, caused him considerable embarrassment, owing to his absence in Edinburgh Castle for a whole year, and that Allan's affairs would naturally be similarly affected.

She had, therefore, a notion that troubles and anxieties might henceforth fall to her lot, and that it would be prudent to delay their intended union for some indefinite period. Her ideas were known to be only too well founded, and in consequence the matter was no longer pressed.

Shortly after this, Flora bade farewell to Lady Margaret and Sir Alexander, and took passage with her brother in a wherry to his residence in the Long Island.

Over the next two years she spent her time in frequent visits to Lady Clanranald at Ormiclade, and other respectable families in the Long Island. On several occasions she crossed to the Isle of Skye, to wait upon her friends at Monkstadt, and particularly to pass months on end with her mother at Armadale.

About this time she appears, from the following letter, to have again visited London. The letter is from her old servant, Niel MacEachainn, who, it will be seen, signs himself *Macdonald:*

Parish, February 28th, 1749. Dear Florry, I've often had it in my head to write you since I parted with you at Edinburgh, but as I did not know how long you stayed there, I was at a loss for a direction, but as yr welfare is always agreeable to me, it gives me pleasure to hear the reason that has brought you back to London. I hope you will make it your endeavour to to deserve as much as in you lyes, the protection of those worthy people that has took you by the hand. I am perfectly acquainted with some of their characters, though I have not the honour to be known to them. The gentleman who delivers this is a friend of mine, and I hope that is enough to make you exert yourself, among the honest and worthy, to help him dispose of some valuable toys he has upon hand. I am sure it must give you a sensible joy to hear the person you once had the honour to Conduct, is in perfect good health. Soon may they enjoy any other blessings the world can give. Clanranald has his kindest compliments to you, and hopes next time you meet, you'll both be in better spirits than when he last saw you. He and I dined with somebody the very day they were took. Good God, what a fright we got! Give yr letters to this gentleman, and believe me, Dear Florry, yr affct friend, and humble servant.

(signed) N. MACDONALD

Flora takes a husband — wedding lasts a week!

At length the time appointed for her marriage arrived, and this event took place at Flodigarry, on November 6, 1750.

It is almost superfluous to say that the wedding festivities were conducted on a large scale, and lasted for the greater part of a week. The company was unusually numerous, and consisted of almost all the gentlemen in Skye and the Long Island, many of them with their ladies.

The bride, robed in a dress of Stuart tartan, with which she was presented when in London by a lady friend, looked remarkably well. All present admired her calm, modest demeanour.

The means adopted to furnish accommodation for such a vast assemblage was both amusing and romantic. An immense barn was fitted up for gentlemen's sleeping berths, while a temporary pavilion was reared, and roofed with heather, to serve alike as a banqueting hall and a ball-room.

It may be remarked, that the expenses connected with

displays of this description, would be naturally looked upon as ruinous to those immediately interested; but nothing of the kind. The customs of the country in those days prevented that.

On occasions of such festivities, even when the parties interested in them were well-to-do, the practice was that the guests privately contributed, as each thought proper, to the cellars and larders of the parties about to be married. In this way all creature comforts of every description, solid and liquid, were furnished on a scale of abundance which was indeed extravagant, and more than sufficient to serve the company, should it be requisite, three times over!

After this happy union, Mr and Mrs Macdonald spent several years in domestic felicity at Flodigarry, where some of their children were born. Old Kingsburgh by this time had become aged and frail, and after his death was succeeded at Kingsburgh by his son, Allan, who moved from Flodigarry. Flora thus became the lady of the mansion where the Prince was sheltered for a night several years before.

Kingsburgh was not an estate or property, as many suppose, but a large farm given first to his factor and afterwards to the factor's son by the proprietor, Sir Alexander Macdonald, at a nominal rent.

Allan Macdonald is said to have been one of the most handsome and powerful Highlanders of his clan, and possessed of all the qualities of body and mind which constitute the real gentleman.

Boswell, whom he entertained with Dr Johnson, describes him as one 'who was completely the figure of a gallant Highlander, exhibiting the graceful mien and manly looks which our popular Scotch song has justly attributed to that character. He had his tartan plaid thrown around him, a large blue bonnet with a knot of black ribbon like a cockade, a brown short coat, tartan waistcoat with gold buttons, a bluish philabeg, and tartan hose.

'He had jet-black hair, tied behind, and was a large stately man, with a steady sensible countenance.'

Such was the man to whom the gallant Flora, then aged 30, yielded her hand and her heart.

Having moved to Kingsburgh, where she spent a considerable part of her married life, she often reflected on the fact that their home was where she had found a night's rest for Prince Charles, and also where she and her husband entertained Dr Johnson, and his friend Boswell, while on their Highland tour in 1773.

'With virtue weighed, what worthless trash is gold?'

The great moralist was evidently much gratified with his reception at this hospitable mansion. He asked Flora as a special favour to be allowed to sleep in the bed which was occupied by the Prince, and his request was cheerfully granted. Not only so, but Flora gave him the identical sheets on which the Prince had lain!

Dr Johnson, who was not at all times easily pleased, was greatly delighted with the kind attention and unobtrusive demeanour of his distinguished hostess, whom he describes as 'A woman of middle stature, soft features, gentle manners, and elegant presence.' This was indeed a great compliment from one who was never known to flatter.

In a letter to his friend, Mr Thrale, he wrote:— 'Flora told me, she thought herself honoured by my visit; and I am sure, whatever regard she bestowed upon me, was liberally repaid. If thou likest her opinion, thou wilt praise her virtues.'

In the morning on which he left Kingsburgh, a slip of paper was found on his toilet table, with these Latin words written in pencil:— *Quantum cedat virtuibus aurum,* which Boswell translated in these terms:— 'With virtue weighed, what worthless trash is gold!' Undoubtedly high praise from the pen of the learned but prejudiced moralist!

At the time of this visit of Johnson and his friend to the

Hebrides, it could no longer be concealed that Kingsburgh, in the face of all his endeavours to the contrary, had become greatly embarrassed in his pecuniary matters. This arose from no mismanagement or extravagance on his part, or on that of his prudent wife, but from heavy losses his father, Kingsburgh, sustained in means and property, serving the Jacobite cause.

The old gentleman's losses and liabilities were very great, and he was much disheartened; and, to add to his misfortunes, he was deprived of the remunerative management, as factor, of his chief's extensive estates. In these distressing matters, Allan became naturally entangled, as his father's representative.

Flora and her husband emigrate to America

At that period, many families from Skye emigrated to America, because of a general depression in the price of cattle, and other circumstances which adversely affected the local economy.

Allan decided to follow his countrymen across the Atlantic, with his wife and family, to build a new life. The embarrassments of her husband only tended to show the true nobleness of Flora's character. She who had risked her life with the Prince was ready and willing to sacrifice everything for a husband's comfort, and to accompany him to whatever quarter of the world it might be expected that fortune would yet smile on the ruined family.

Consequently, in the month of August, 1774, Kingsburgh and family sailed in the ship *Baliol*, from Campbeltown, Kintyre, to North Carolina.

They had a very favourable passage. The time of their departure from Scotland became known among their countrymen in Carolina where they were anxioulsy expected and joyfuly received on their arrival. Flora's fame preceded her for years; and her countrymen felt proud of the prospect of having her in their community.

Various demonstrations, on a large scale, were made to welcome her to American territory. Soon after her landing, a largely attended ball was given in her honour at Wilmington, where she was gratified by the great attention paid to her daughter Anne, then entering into womanhood, a young lady of surpassing beauty.

An American gentleman, speaking of Flora's reception on this occasion, says, that 'on her arrival at Cross Creek she received a truly Highland welcome from her old neighbours and kinsfolk, who had crossed the Atlantic years before her. The strains of the *Piobaireachd,* and the martial airs of her native land, greeted her on her approach to the capital of the Scottish Settlement. In that village she remained for some time visiting and receiving visits from friends, while her husband went to the western part of Cumberland in quest of land.'

She spent about six months in Cameron's Hill, in Cumberland, where she and her family were regular worshippers in a Presbyterian Church at Long Street, under the pastoral care of a countryman, the Rev Mr Macleod.

In 1775 her daughter, Anne, became the wife of Major Alexander Macleod of Glendale, Moor County, a gallant youth and a Skyeman, who subsequently distinguished himself in the European wars, and rose to the rank of Major-General in the British service.

Mrs Major-General Macleod (that is, Flora's daughter, Anne) died in the house of her daughter, Mary, at the village of Stein, in Skye, in 1834. She was a highly accomplished, most agreeable old lady, and she delighted to give minute details of the adventures of her distinguished mother.

Her eldest son, an officer in the army, happened to be at Fort George on the occasion of a Northern Meeting Ball in Inverness, which he attended, when a dispute arose between himself and Glengarry. This led to a duel, in which poor Macleod was killed.

The family is caught up in Independence Wars

Unfortunately for Flora and her family, on their arrival in the New World the American War of Independence was just starting and young Kingsburgh soon became involved.

In 1775, Governor Martin raised from among the Scotch Highlanders a body of men to be sent to Boston, and mustered them into the Royal Highland Emigrant Regiment. Seeing the distinction and honour which all classes of Highlanders awarded to Flora and her husband Kingsburgh, the crafty Governor gave him the chief command of Brigadier-General, an honour which proved a deep source of grief to Flora.

'In order to assemble the Scots,' says an American writer, 'balls were given in different parts of the settlement, some of which Flora attended, with her daughter, Mrs Major Macleod, and her younger daughter Fanny. Upon these occasions, Anne and Fanny reigned supreme, and bore off the honours of the ball-room.'

Early in January, 1776, Allan Macdonald bought a tract of land from Caleb Touchstone, on the borders of Richmond and Montgomery Counties, and named the place Killiegray. While residing here, a severe typhus fever attacked the younger members of the family, and two of Flora's children died, a boy and a girl, aged respectively 11 and 13.

To add to the mother's grief, her husband was absent at his official duties, and was not permitted even to attend the funeral of his beloved children. A subsequent owner of Killiegray fenced in the graves of these children, to preserve the spot sacred to the memory of Flora's offspring.

When the royal banner was unfurled at Cross Creek in 1776, and the loyalist army marched towards Brunswick, under the command of General Donald Macdonald, Allan of Kingsburgh had his own duties allotted to him as Brigadier-General. Flora, with the due devotion of an affectionate wife, followed her husband for many days, and encamped one night with him in a dangerous place, on the brow of Haymount, near the Arsenal of the United States.

For a time she would not listen to her husband's earnest entreaties that she should return home, as his own life was enough to be in jeopardy. Next morning, however, when the army took up its line of march, midst banners streaming in the breeze, and martial music floating on the air, Flora deemed it high time to retrace her steps.

She affectionately embraced her husband, and her eyes were dimmed with tears as she breathed to heaven a fervent prayer for his safe and speedy return to his family and home. But alas! she never saw him again in America.

Who can conceive the many anxious days and sleepless nights that the spirited heroine passed in these turbulent and bloody times, afraid that every messenger who arrived was a messenger to announce the death of her gallant husband?

Captured at Moore's Creek and sent to jail

Later the defeat of the loyalist army, and the capture of her husband at Moore's Creek, broke her heart. The officers were arrested and imprisoned, and Kingsburgh was committed to the prison of Halifax, Virginia.

By now few of her family were around to comfort her. Her five sons were absent, engaged in the service of their country. Her daughter Anne, Major MacLeod's wife, was settled in a house of her own, and her daughter Fanny, still in precarious health, from the dregs of the recent fever, was too young to sympathise with a mother in deep distress.

After many difficulties she decided, on the recommendation of her imprisoned husband, to return, if possible, to Scotland. An officer friend of the family helped with the necessary documentation and Flora set sail for home in 1779, leaving her husband still a prisoner in Halifax Jail.

Crossing the Atlantic, with none of her family but Fanny, the gallant Flora met with the last of her adventures. The vessel in which she sailed was met by a French privateer, and a skirmish blew up.

During the engagement Flora refused to take shelter below, but prominently appeared on deck, where she inspired the sailors with courage, and assured them of success. Unfortunately her left arm was broken in the conflict, and she was afterwards accustomed to say that she had fought both for the House of Stuart and the House of Hanover, but had been 'wounded' in the service of each.

Flora had seven children — five sons and two daughters — besides three who died young. All her sons were officers who distinguished themselves in the service of their king and country.

Charles, the eldest, was a captain in the Queen's Rangers, and was a very accomplished man. Alexander, the second, was a captain of marines, and of high professional character.

James, the fourth, served in the Tarleton British Legion, and was a brave officer. John, the fifth, was a lieutenant-colonel, and had a numerous family.

Her daughters, on the other hand, became the wives of officers. Anne, as has been said, was the wife of Major-General Alexander Macleod. Her second daughter, Fanny, married Lieutenant Donald Macdonald, of Cuiderach, in Skye.

Following Flora's return from America, after an absence of five years, she kept up a considerable correspondence with friends in different quarters of the country. Two of her letters written in 1780 and 1782, are preserved in the Jacobite Memoirs. These were penned while her husband was still in Halifax prison, and her sons still engaged in the service of her country. She was then about sixty years of age.

Secrets of Flora's letters

The letters are valuable, as they show that she was an accomplished woman, an affectionate mother, and a devoted wife. They show further, that the source of her cheerful temper and serenity of mind was a steadfast, well-grounded faith in God.

The two letters preserved, were addressed to the wife of the late Sir Alexander Muir Mackenzie, of Delvin, near Dunkeld. Flora's son, Alexander, when a boy, lived for nearly three years with this family, where he was treated as if he had been one of their own.

The first is in the following terms:—

DUNVEGAN, SKYE, 12th July, 1780

DEAR MADAM, – I arrived at Inverness the third day after parting with you, in good health, and without any accidents, which I always dread. My young squire continued always very obliging and attentive to me. I staid at Inverness for three days. I had the good luck to meet with a female companion from that to Skye. I was the fourth day, with great difficulty, at Raasay, for my hands being so pained with the riding.

I have arrived here a few days ago with my young daughter, who promises to be a stout Highland 'Caileag', quite overgrown for her age. Nanny and her family are well. Her husband was not sailed the last account she had from him.

I have the pleasure to inform you, upon my arrival here, that I had two letters from my husband, the latter dated 10th May. He was then in very good health, and informs me that my son Charles has got the command of a troop of horse in Lord Cathcart's regiment; but alas! I have heard nothing since I left you about my son Sandy, which, you may be sure, gives me great uneasiness. But I still hope for the best.

By public and private news I hope we will soon have peace re-established, to our great satisfaction. which, as it's a thing long expected and wished for, will be for the utility of the whole nation — especially to poor me, that has my all engaged. Fond to hear news, and yet afraid to get it.

I wait here till a favourable opportunity for the Long Island shall offer itself. As I am upon all occasions under the greatest obligations to you, should you get a letter from my son Johnnie sooner than I would get one from him, you would very much oblige me by dropping me a few lines communicating to me the most material part of this letter.

I hope you and the ladies of your family will accept of my kindest respects, and I ever am, with esteem,

Dear Madadm, your affectionate, humble servant,

FLORA MACDONALD

P.S. — Please direct to me, to Mrs Macdonald, late of Kingsbarrow, South Uist, by Dunvegan.

To Mrs Mackenzie of Delvin, by Dunkeld.

The second reads: —

DEAR MADAM, — I received your agreeable favour a fortnight ago. and I am happy to find your health is not worse than when I left you. I return you my most sincere thanks for your being so mindful of me as to send me the agreeable news about Johny's arrival, which relieved me of a great deal of distress, as that was the first accounts I had of him since he sailed. I think, poor man, he has been very lucky for getting into bread so soon after landing. I had a letter from John which, I suppose, came by the same conveyance with yours. I am told by others that it will be in his power to show his talents, as being in the engineer department. He speaks feelingly of the advantages he got in his youth. and the good example show'd him, which I hope will keep him from doing anything that is either sinful or shameful.

I received a letter from Captain Macdonald, my husband, dated from Halifax, the 12th Nov '81. He was then recovering his health. but had been very tender for some time before. My son. Charles, is captain in the British Legion, and James a lieutenant in the same. They are both in New York. Ranald is captain of Marines. and was with Rodney at the taking of St Eustati. As for my son Sandy who was amissing I had accounts of his being carried to Lisbon, but nothing certain, which I look upon, on the whole, as a hearsay; but the kindness of Providence is still to be looked upon, as I have no reason to complain, as God has been pleased to spare his father and the rest. I am now in my brother's house, on my way to Skye, to attend my daughter, who is to ly-in in August. They are all in health at present. As for my health at present, it's tolerable, considering my anxious mind and distress of times.

It gives me a great deal of pleasure to hear such good accounts of young Mr Mackenzie. No doubt he has a great debt to pay who represents his worthy and amiable uncle. I hope you will be so good as to remember me to your female companions. I do not despair of the pleasure of seeing you once more, if peace was restored; and I am, dear Madam, with

The sad last wish
of Flora Macdonald

When peace was eventually restored, Flora's husband was freed from Halifax jail, and he made as little delay as possible in returning to Skye, as Captain on half-pay.

On his arrival at Portree, he was met by his affectionate wife, and a numerous party of friends. He made no delay in reaching Kingsburgh

For eight or nine years Flora and her husband lived comfortably and happily in their old residence, until both were removed by death, within less than two years of each other.

On March 5, 1790, the ever-memorable Flora departed this life. She died following a short illness and retained to the last that vivacity of character, and amiableness of disposition, by which she was distinguished throughout her life.

Her death took place at Peinduin, a friend's house on the sea coast, about three miles north of Kingsburgh. She went there in her usual health, to pay a friendly visit to the family, but was taken suddenly ill with an inflammatory complaint.

The doctors were unable to treat her. She possessed all her mental faculties to the very last, and calmly departed in the presence of her husband and two daughters.

Flora's remains were shrouded in one of the sheets in which the Prince had slept at the mansion of Kingsburgh. In all her travels she had never parted from it It was religiously and faithfully preserved by her in North Carolina, during the War. She had it in safe keeping even when her own person was in danger.

At length the purpose she intended it for was accomplished, when all that was mortal of herself was wrapt in it by her sorrowing family.

Her remains were conveyed under shade of night from Peinduin to Kingsburgh. The coffin was carried shoulder-high by a party of stalwart youths procured for the purpose.

The night was pitch-dark, except when frequent flashes of lightning spread a momentary gleam over the scene. Thunder rolled with terrific peals; rain fell in gushing torrents.

It would seem as if the ghosts and hob-goblins had that night left their dark abodes to take a 'dander' abroad, to lash up the elements into a perfect fury!

At that time there were no roads or bridges in Skye. When the funeral party arrived at the river of Hinisdale, about half the journey, it was swollen from bank to bank. The usual ford was impracticable, while higher up it was, if possible, worse.

Some proposed to return, while others objected, stating that she whose body they carried never flinched when alive, from any duty which she had undertaken, neither would they flinch from performing their last duties to her mortal remains.

After due consultation, it was agreed to attempt crossing by the strand near the sea beach, and this was safely accomplished. Shortly after they reached Kingsburgh, where the body lay in state for nearly a week.

At length the funeral day arrived. The procession started at an early hour, as the distance between Kingsburgh and the place of burial was about sixteen miles.

The body was interred in the churchyard of Kilmuir, in the

north end of Skye, within a square piece of coarse wall, erected in 1776, to enclose the tombs of the Kingsburgh family.

The funeral cortege was immense — more than a mile in length — consisting of several thousands of every rank in Skye and the adjacent Isles.

Flora's marriage and funeral, between which there was an interval of forty years, were the most numerously attended of any of which there is any record in the Western Isles.

Notwithstanding the vast assemblage present, all were liberally supplied with every variety of refreshment. Of genuine 'mountain dew' alone upwards of three hundred gallons were served.

About a dozen of pipers from the MacCrimmon and MacArthur colleges in Skye, and from other quarters, simultaneously played the 'Coronach', the usual melancholy lament for departed greatness.

And thus ended a marvellous life and a famous chapter in Scotland's story.